100% PALLET

from freight to furniture

21 DIY DESIGNER PROJECTS

AURÉLIE DROUET

photography JÉRÔME BLIN

SCRIPTUM
EDITIONS

CONTENTS

DESIGNS

DESIGNER PROFILES

INTRODUCTION

While pallets have frequently inspired visual artists of all persuasions, over the past few years they have excited a particular interest among interior designers, and especially among furniture designers.

Recycling pallets to make furniture is a manifestation of the 'eco-design' movement that has made this everyday packaging the raw material of choice for anyone wanting to make their own distinctive and original furniture, simply and at little cost. Easy to dismantle and to stack, pallets offer a multitude of opportunities for making your own bespoke furniture.

This is the concept that unites and inspires the designers in this book, who have brought together an array of furniture that is practical, functional and simple to create. The techniques of construction and assembly they use are clearly thought out and explained with care in order to make the process as accessible as possible. None of the projects featured here requires any specialist skills or materials; all of them by contrast – thanks to handy technical tips, plans and illustrated step-by-step instructions – are simple to understand and easy to make.

It is an approach that echoes the work of the great Italian designer Enzo Mari (who in 1974 embarked on his *Proposta per un'autoprogettazione*, later published as *Autoprogettazione?*): 'I thought that if people were encouraged to build a table with their own hands, they would be in a position to understand the thinking that lay behind it.'

From a child's bed to an armchair, via a sun lounger, wall lights and much more, the projects here encompass all the fundamentals of pallet furniture, encapsulated in ideas that are designed to be borrowed and adapted to suit any taste and every setting.

TIPS AND POINTERS

To make the designs

For each design you will find a list of the tools and materials required to make it. As the basic toolkit is not repeated each time, here is a list of the tools that you will need to keep to hand:

- a metre rule
- a good carpenter's pencil
- a metal rule and square
- gloves, safety spectacles and mask
- a slotted screwdriver and Phillips screwdriver
- hammers (various sizes)
- pliers (various)
- paintbrushes: round, sash, flat, mini-roller
- a power sander (various grades of sandpaper)
- a power drill (various drill bits)

Measurements concerning the size of nails, screws and nuts is for guidance only, to be adapted according to the thickness of the boards you are working with.

In each case an indication of the type and dimensions of the pallets used is given, but every design can also be made using different sorts of pallet. The plans are designed to be adapted to whatever type of pallets you happen to find.

Safety warning: electrical installations of all kinds require special care, especially on wooden supports. For your safety, always check the product specifications with your retailer, and when in doubt seek professional advice.

To create your own designs

Each design proposed here is a basic model from which you can improvise your own designs. Use them for inspiration to create your own variations.

Readers are invited to send photos of their own designs inspired by this book to the author at: aureledrouet@free.fr

A POTTED HISTORY OF THE PALLET

Where can you find pallets? What type of pallets should you look for? Returnable or single-use? Treated or untreated?

Jean Dossin, President of the Syndicat de l'Industrie et des Services de la Palette (Sypal), and Patrice Chanrion, Director of Marketing and Communications of the PGS Group answer these questions and more.

What is the story of the wooden pallet?

The pallet came into being in America in the 1930s. During the Second World War, the US government encouraged and greatly expanded their use for the transportation and storage of equipment in vast quantities. By the late 1940s, many American industries used them in order to remain competitive and successful. European industry took a while longer to grasp the advantages of using palettes, and although a handful of pioneers started using them in the 1950s, they did not reach their full potential until the 1970s. The reconditioning of pallets is a more recent development, by contrast, emerging only in 1975–80, in response on the one hand to the fact that users want to be free of the constraints of returnable pallets, and on the other

to the need to economize on raw materials in the wake of the first oil crisis.

What are the main kinds of pallet? Are there standard types?

The wooden pallet has become an indispensable tool throughout the supply chain, for the assembly, stacking, storage, handling and transportation of goods and merchandise. It is used in every sector of industry, including food processing, engineering, chemicals, construction, pharmaceuticals and automobiles. In response to the varied needs of their clients, pallet manufacturers make a number of different types, divided into groups according to their use:

- **Four-way (heavy or 'block') pallets:** designed to be re-used and built to last, these are more robust than pallets for limited use.

- **Two-way (light or 'stringer') pallets:** designed for limited use, these pallets are in theory disposable. In practice, many are re-used several times and repaired as necessary. These pallets are often 'made to measure', to answer a client's specific needs.

- **Standard pallets:** built to French, European or international standards, in practice these pallets are exclusively four-way.

- **Euro pallets:** developed in 1950, on the initiative of international rail freight companies, these pallets measuring 800 (2'7½") x 1200mm (3'11¼") were designed according to highly precise specifications. Subsequently adopted by 18 European rail networks, they became known as the 'Euro pallet'. Until 1995, the SNCF was one of the bodies enforcing these standards. Since then, the European Pallet Association (EPAL) has taken over responsibility for the EUR-EPAL brand.

- **Other pallets:** other commonly found standard pallets include CP pallets, used by the chemical industry; VMF pallets, used by the glass industry; cement pallets; and galia pallets, used by the car industry.

What is a 'returnable' pallet?

This description may mean several things. First, a pallet is returnable if it forms part of a pool that defines legal appurtenance (such as ecoPGS pallets, relocalisation systems of the PAKi type, or hired pallets). This is also the case with exchangeable Euro pallets, and with pools dedicated to a single industry (such as VMF – *Verreries Mécaniques de France* – pallets). All of these pallets are distinguished by their colour, initials or a variety of other markings. In theory, they should all be returned to their owners after use.

What is the life cycle of a pallet?

Used pallets go through a number of different processes. According to their condition, some may need repairs and others will be beyond repair; most, however, will not need repairing. When a pallet is damaged, on average two or even three elements are replaced; beyond this, the cost of the repairs outweighs any potential profit from putting it back into circulation. In 60 to 70% of cases, repairs are carried out with 'new lumber'; for the remainder, repairs may be carried out using wood salvaged from pallets that are broken beyond repair and moulded wood blocks.

Which woods are used to make pallets?

In the absence of any particular specifications, standards or legislative constraints, most common types of wood may be used in packaging. In practice, however, the number of species used remains small. Five are used for the manufacture of pallets: poplar, maritime pine, Scots pine, spruce and Douglas fir.

Where can you find pallets for personal use?

There are many possibilities, but since in normal circumstances they should never be abandoned on the public highway, you will always need to apply to the holder, whether this be a major DIY store, supermarket, convenience store, building site, market, exhibition centre or pallet reconditioning firm.

In order to recycle pallets to make furniture you need to take certain precautions, especially with regard to any treatments. How can you tell the difference between treated and untreated pallets?

In climatic conditions that encourage the development of mould and for species of naturally low durability, it may be necessary to apply a preservative. The treatments are selected according to the intended purpose of the pallets and their effectiveness is

recognized by official regulating bodies. These will accept only treatments that respect the quality of the food chain, health requirements and environmental factors. In France, the *Direction Générale de la Concurrence, de la Consommation et de la Répression des Fraudes* publishes a summary of treatments permitted for wood that will come into contact with fruit and vegetables. In order to avoid using chemical treatments, manufacturers are now developing successful artificial drying techniques.

Some pallets may have been treated in the past by fumigation with methyl bromide (MB), a toxic gas that was banned in 2010. Pallets marked MB are therefore to be avoided. To be on the safe side, use pallets marked with an ear of corn and the letters HT (Heat Treatment), indicating a natural, non-adjuvant treatment in which, before it can be exported to certain countries, the wood is heated to a minimum core temperature of 56°C for at least 30 minutes. Pallets that do not need to be treated for their intended use are left unmarked.

In order to be sure that the pallets you are salvaging are clean and wholesome, avoid any that are stained with paint or any other hard-to-identify products. Choose your source with care, and if possible go to a firm that reconditions pallets and will be able to advise you. Finally, furniture made using pallets is usually sanded or even planed, which all helps to get rid of any treatment that might be present.

A POCKET GLOSSARY

Block or stringer, reversible or double-face? Standard or otherwise, pallets come in numerous different variants. Without getting too technical, here is a concise rundown of pallet terminology.

Block: squat deck-spacer, rectangular or cylindrical in section, positioned beneath the top deck or between the top and bottom decks, leaving room for the passage of fork truck tines or for pallet jacks.

Bottom board: board forming part of the bottom deck of the pallet.

Bottom deck: flat horizontal surface formed by arrangement of deckboards and spreading the load on the ground.

Crosspiece: horizontal board joining the blocks to the top deckboards.

Double-deck pallet: flat pallet with upper and lower decks.

Four-way entry pallet: pallet allowing entry to fork truck tines on all four sides.

Non-reversible pallet: flat double-deck pallet of which only one deck can be loaded.

Notch: section cut out of lower part of the stringer to allow entry for the fork truck tines, perpendicular to the stringers.

Notched stringer pallet: pallet with stringers notched to allow entry of fork truck tines.

Reversible pallet: flat pallet with identical top and bottom decks that be loaded on either side.

Single-deck pallet: flat pallet with a single deck.

Stringer: continuous longitudinal beam-component of the pallet supporting the top deck or positioned between the top and bottom deck.

Top deck: flat surface consisting of an arrangement of deckboards and forming the upper load-carrying surface of the pallet.

Two-way entry pallet: pallet allowing entry to fork truck tines from the two ends only.

Wing: part of deckboard(s) overhanging the outside edge of the stringers or blocks, designed to aid lifting by cranes.

.

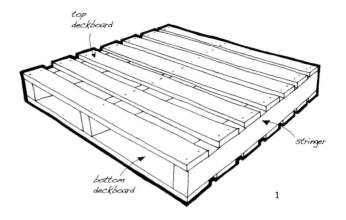

top deckboard

stringer

bottom deckboard

1

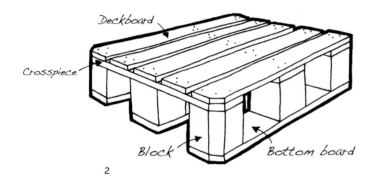

Deckboard

Crosspiece

Block

Bottom board

2

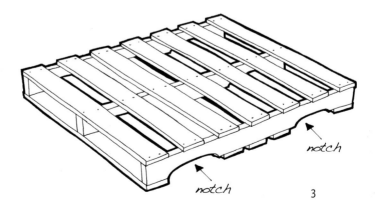

notch

notch

3

1. Stringer pallet
2. Block pallet
3. Notched stringer pallet

1.

2.

3.

4.

5.

6.

TOOL GUIDE

(1) Staple gun

A hand-held staple gun is the ideal tool for all finishing work. Light and compact, it can be used to affix different surfaces rapidly and accurately. The action is more controlled that that of a hammer, with less risk of splitting the wood. It also allows the use of specific nails such as lost-head or round-head pins, so as to give a neat and professional finish.

(3) Angle grinder

Blocks and stringers are too thick for removing nails with a hammer. If pliers or a nail wrench can't reach the most awkward ones, try using an angle grinder. Its metal disc shears off nails flush with the wood. Be careful not to hold it too close to the surface, when it can leave black marks or grooves. Safety spectacles, gloves and ear defenders are essential.

(5) Jigsaw

To guarantee that you get the best use out of your jigsaw, make sure you choose one that can cut different thicknesses of wood, has variable speed and an adjustable base plate (up to 45 degrees) for making cuts on sloping surfaces. Choose the right blades for the material you want to saw. Observe the necessary safety precautions, and the jigsaw will enable you to work accurately and safely.

(2) Mitre box

U-shaped in section, with notches for making 45-degree and 90-degree cuts, the mitre box is an indispensible tool for carpentry. Although the tenon saw (backsaw) is associated with this tool, a handsaw with a blade fine enough to fit in the notches can also be used. Position the piece of wood in the box and hold it firmly in place, then slide the saw blade into the notches to either side of it, according to the angle you want to achieve.

(4) Mitre saw

Less expensive than the power version, the hand mitre saw allows you to make very accurate cuts at 30, 45, 60 and 90 degrees. To obtain the best cut, choose a saw that can hold the wood still. An entry-level tool suitable for everyday DIY projects will cost £20-30 ($30-45).

(6) Detail sander

The detail or corner sander is a vibrating sander that is ideal for finishing. The shape and small dimensions of its sanding surface make it highly practical for sanding small areas that are flat but 'distressed' and for reaching difficult spots, and it is both light and very easy to use.

HOW TO DISMANTLE A WOODEN PALLET

Dismantling a wooden pallet requires patience, care and a good deal of elbow grease. The method you choose will depend on the tools you have to hand and the type of pallet you are working with.

Method 1: brick bolster (1 and 2)
With a brick bolster, you can slice through the nails between the boards. Insert it between the deckboards and the stringers or blocks, according to the type of pallet, then strike it with a hammer.

Method 2: crow bar and hammer (3 and 4)
This is the method used for dismantling block pallets. Using a tapping block to spread the blows and avoid damaging the wood, strike the blocks in turn in order to loosen them slightly. Insert the hammer between the block and the crosspiece, then use it as a lever. Repeat with the crow bar to dismantle completely.

Method 3: hacksaw (5)
Insert the hacksaw blade between the deckboards and the stringers or blocks, according to the type of pallet, and saw through the nails. If the gap is too small, use a small screwdriver to lever the two surfaces apart.

What to do with the nails?
According to the finish you want for your piece of furniture, you have two possibilities.

1. Remove them
If the nails have been sawn, use a nail punch, a small hammer and pliers to remove them. Position the nail punch over the sawn end of the nail, then strike it gently with the hammer to force it out through the other side. Turn the board over and pull the nail out with pliers. If the nails are still whole, bang the points to push them out, then remove them with pliers. Use wood filler to fill the holes.

2. Keep them (6)
Use a hacksaw or an angle grinder to shear off any protruding points.

As you go through this book you will see that in our designs we have preferred to keep the nails, as we believe they form an integral part of the pallet aesthetic.

1.

2.

3.

4.

5.

6.

THE SANDMAN
CHILD'S BED

A child's bedroom is the reflection of their world, of their universe. This is where they sleep, play and wake up in the morning. This is their space, furnished to give them a sense of wellbeing — and no piece of furniture is more important than the bed. For our little ones, whose sleep is so important as they grow, their bed must be comfortable and welcoming, promising peaceful slumbers and sweet dreams. *The Sandman* offers the ideal solution for a gentle transition from cot to a big bed. Your child will feel snugly cocooned in this wooden nest with its many nooks for stowing treasures.

The Sandman symbolizes sleep, evoking the figure of folklore who sprinkles magic sand onto children's eyes in order to lull them to sleep.

DESIGN INSPIRED BY:
LORI DANELLE

MADE BY:
AURÉLIE DROUET & JÉRÔME BLIN

THE SANDMAN **CHILD'S BED**

TOOLBOX

Tools

- Tools
- Jigsaw
- Handsaw
- Hammer
- Flat spanner
- Screw gun
- Angle grinder
- Clamps
- Small foam paint roller
- Round paintbrush

Materials

- 2 900 (2'11½") x 1100mm (3'7⅓") double-deck stringer pallets
- 2 600 (23½") x 800mm (2'7½") block pallets with butt-jointed top deck
- Double-threaded wood screws
- Nails
- 3 nuts and washers (ø8 (⁵⁄₁₆") x 80mm (3¼"))
- 5 swivel castors, including 1 braked (75mm (3") diameter)
- Wood paint in a colour of your choice

Telling details: Storage spaces in the bed head and under the base.
Swivel castors mean you can move the bed easily.

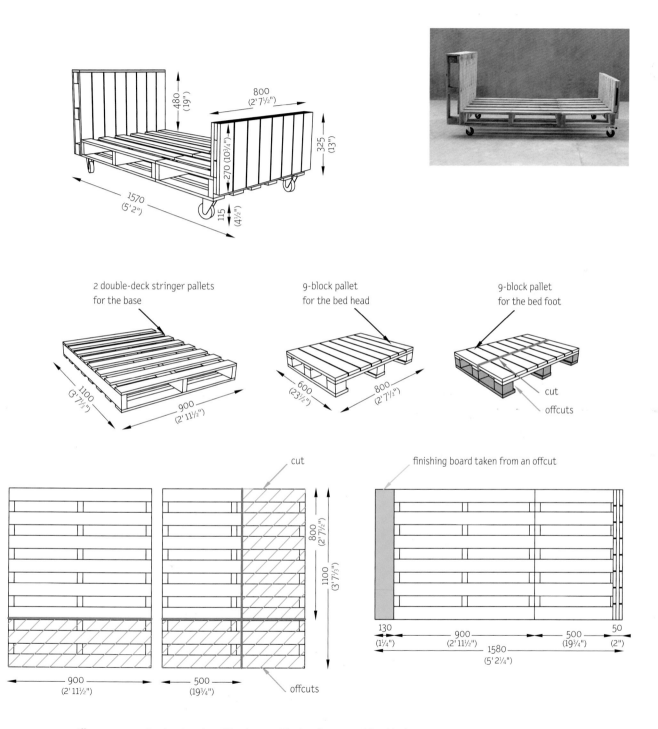

480
(19")

800
(2' 7½")

270 (10¾")

325
(13")

1570
(5' 2")

115
(4½")

2 double-deck stringer pallets
for the base

9-block pallet
for the bed head

9-block pallet
for the bed foot

1100
(3' 7⅓")

900
(2' 11½")

600
(23½")

800
(2' 7½")

cut

offcuts

cut

finishing board taken from an offcut

800
(2' 7½")

1100
(3' 7⅓")

offcuts

900
(2' 11½")

500
(19¾")

130
(1¼")

900
(2' 11½")

500
(19¾")

50
(2")

1580
(5' 2¼")

All measurements are given in millimetres and inches (to nearest fraction)

Method

1. To make the base, cut the 2 stringer pallets to the dimensions shown on the plan (to obtain a bed 800 (2'7½") x 1400mm (4'7⅛")). Sand, ideally, with a power sander.

2. The bed foot is made from the 600 (23½") x 800mm (2'7½") block pallet, keeping only the top deck. Dismantle the bottom deck and blocks according to method 2, p.16.

3. Grind down the protuding nails using the angle grinder.

4. Using a handsaw, saw down the deck along the central crosspiece.

5. Place the two sections on top of each other, back to back, aligning the narrower section on one of the crosspieces.

6. Nail together the two parts of the bed foot, then sand.

7. For the bed head, use the second block pallet whole. Salvage an offcut board 800mm (2'7½") long and of a width to match the depth of the block pallet. Nail it to the blocks, then sand the bed head.

8. Join the stringers of the 2 pallets forming the base using 3 nuts. Drill a hole in the centre and one at each end of the stringer of the first pallet, using a wood drill bit of the same diameter as the nuts.

9. Place the 2 pallets on the ground, upside-down, and hold them in position using clamps on the stringers. Insert the drill into the holes, then drill through into the second stringer.

10. Put the nuts and washers in place, then tighten them the spanner.

11. Screw in the 4 swivel castors, one braked, at each corner of the bed. Screw the fifth one in the centre of the stringers joining the two pallets. Turn the base over.

12. Clamping it securely in place, screw the bed foot to the base.

13. Clamping it securely in place, screw the bed head to the base.

14. Apply the paint, using the small foam roller on the flat surfaces and the round brush to finish.

15. With its swivel castors, the bed is easy to move. Use the braked castor to immobilize it when your child is playing on it or sleeping.

16. Use the gaps in the pallet as shelves for bedtime stories, so creating a private library in the bed head.

MAN'S BEST FRIEND
FLOOR LAMP

Though highly practical, this tongue-in-cheek reference to
man's best friend refuses to take itself seriously. The *Man's
Best Friend* lamp is not merely decorative, but is also designed
to shed a specific light in a specific location, with a light level
that is carefully calculated. Standing in the living room, beside
a screen, it sheds an atmospheric light that is neither too
intense nor too discreet, but is simple and effective.

Designed to stand by the arm of a sofa, it also serves as
a shelf for remote controls and magazines. Why the name?
As it came together, its boards became paws and its electric
cable a tail. And it can move around just like a pet curled up
beside the sofa.

DESIGN:
PHILIPPE DANEY

MAN'S BEST FRIEND FLOOR LAMP

TOOLBOX

Tools

- Screwdriver
- Detail sander + sanding block
- Cloth
- Flat paintbrush

Materials

- 1 530 (21") x 310mm (12½") offcut from a reversible stringer pallet (here from the *Charles-Edouard* armchair)
- aluminium strip
- 1 LED strip light kit (comprising LED strip, connectors and transformer)
- Methylated spirits
- 8 small wood screws
- Wood paint in a colour of your choice

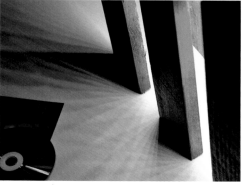

Telling details: Simple and quick to make.
Subtle lighting for a perfect ambience.

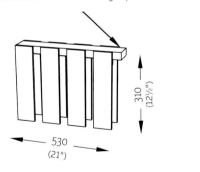

310
(12½")

530
(21")

offcut from a reversible stringer pallet

310
(12½")

530
(21")

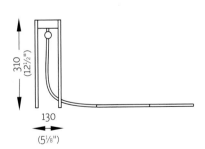

310
(12½")

130
(5⅛")

All measurements are given in millimetres and inches (to nearest fraction)

Method

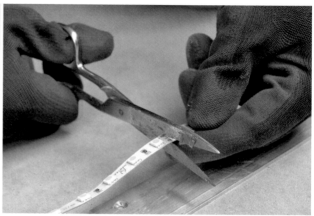

1. Sand the pallet, using a sanding block for the inner face of the stringer.

2. Cut 390mm (15⅓") of the aluminium strip. Cut the LED strip to the same length, following the cutting guides on the strip. **Safety warning:** *follow the instructions with the LED strip; if in doubt, consult a professional.*

3. Wipe the aluminum strip with methylated spirits in order to ensure better adhesion for the self-adhesive LED strip.

4. Carefully stick the LED strip on to the aluminium strip.

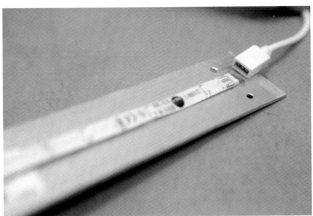

5. Connect the transformer connectors to the LED strip. Nowadays manufacturers provide simplified connections in which each element has its own easily recognizable plug.

6. Centre the aluminum strip on the stringer and screw it down.

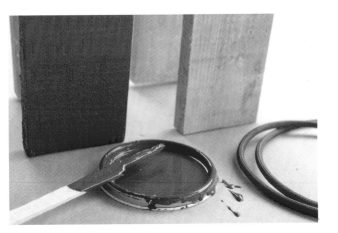

7. To finish, paint with one or two coats of paint, according to the desired result. Wood is a porous surface that quickly absorbs paint. To economize on paint you can use a special wood undercoat to first seal the wood.

CHARLES-EDOUARD
ARMCHAIR

With its cubist lines and timeless design, the *Charles-Edouard* armchair encapsulates the art of simplicity. Its classic aesthetic – demanding a splash of bold colour – will complement any interior.

The name of the *Charles-Edouard* armchair is a reference to Charles-Édouard Jeanneret-Gris, better known as Le Corbusier. For this design, Martin and Mathieu took their inspiration from the architect's famous LC2 armchair with its defining structure – in chrome for the LC2, in wooden pallets for the *Charles-Edouard*.

DESIGN:
M&M DESIGNERS
CUSHIONS:
MARIE-NOËLLE SALAÜN

CHARLES-EDOUARD ARMCHAIR

TOOLBOX

Tools

- Handsaw
- Jigsaw
- Adjustable square or flat metal square
- Orbital sander and detail sander
- Screw gun
- Clamps
- 1 small paint roller
- 1 small round paintbrush
- 1 flat paintbrush

Materials

- 2 1150 (3'9¼") x 1150mm (3'9¼") reversible stringer pallets
- Double-threaded wood screws
- 4 80 (3¼")/80 (3¼")/40mm (1½") angle braces
- 6 40 (1½")/40 (1½")/40mm (1½") angle braces
- Wood paint in a colour of your choice
- 80mm (3¼") cushion foam, plus fabric for covers

Telling details: Space for storage in the arms.
An adventurous colour scheme to offset the classic aesthetic.

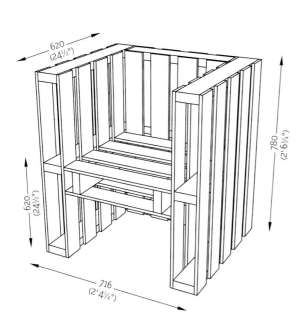

620
(24½")

780
(2' 6¾")

620
(24½")

716
(2' 4¼")

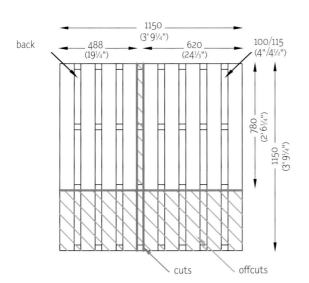

back

1150
(3' 9¼")

488
(19¼")

620
(24⅓")

100/115
(4"/4½")

780
(2' 6¾")

1150
(3' 9¼")

cuts

offcuts

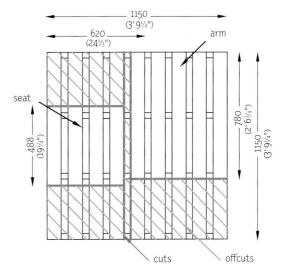

1150
(3' 9¼")

arm

620
(24⅓")

seat

488
(19¼")

780
(2' 6¾")

1150
(3' 9¼")

cuts

offcuts

All measurements are given in millimetres and inches (to nearest fraction)

Method

1. Mark out the measurements from the plan on both pallets, then saw them. As the pallets are reversible, be careful to mark them out on both sides for the most accurate results.

2. You will then have the four sections of the chair: the seat and one arm from the first pallet, and the back and the other arm from the second.

3. Sand all the sections, ideally, with a power sander.

4. Use a detail sander for the stringers and the edges of the boards. Small and triangular in shape, this is a useful tool for sanding small areas and reaching awkward spots.

5. Paint the sections before assembling them. Use a small roller for the boards and chevrons, a flat brush for the inner face of the pallets, and a round brush for finishing. Do not dilute the paint, and use two coats, sanding lightly between each coat.

6. Place the flat metal square on the ground. Using this as a guide, form a right angle between the back and the first arm, then clamp them in position.

7. Position the seat at the desired height (here 400mm (15¾"), to align with the stringers of the arms) and mark out a rough line along the bottom edge.

8. Using this line as a guide, screw on 4 angle braces (80 (3¼")/80 (3¼")/40mm (1½")) to assemble the back and arms.

9. Place the chair on its back, then clamp the seat in position at the desired height. Use the square to check the accuracy of the angles.

10. Screw 2 angle braces (40 (1½") /40 (1½") /40mm (1½")) to the seat and back.

11. Screw 4 angle braces (40 (1½") /40 (1½") /40mm (1½")) to the seat and arms.

12. To make the cushions, measure the internal dimensions of the seat and back, then cut pads from the 80mm (3¼") foam. Take care when cutting the back cushion, as it rests on the seat cushion, so the height should be reduced by 80mm (3¼").

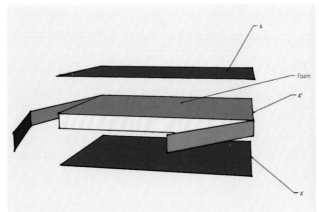

13. For each cover, cut 2 fabric rectangles of equal sizes (A and A') to match the dimensions of the foam, adding 10mm (⁷⁄₁₆") on each side for the seams. Then cut out a strip (A") to form the sides of the cushion.

14. Place one of the rectangles of fabric and the side strip edge to edge, then sew together on three sides; repeat with the other rectangle. Turn the cover right way out and insert the foam pad. Sew up the opening using slipstitch.

15. The spaces in the arms are useful for storing books and magazines.

Nina Tolstrup
Studiomama

Nina Tolstrup
in 5 dates

1962: Born in Copenhagen, Denmark.

2000: Sets up Studiomama.

2010: Nominated in the furniture category of the Brit Insurance Design of the Year award.

2010: *Pallet Project* show at the Phillips de Pury Gallery, New York.

2011: Exhibition at the Libby Sellers Gallery, London.

Nina Tolstrup is international: Danish by birth, she studied in Paris at the Ecole Nationale Supérieure de Création Industrielle (ENSCI-Les Ateliers), before moving to London and setting up Studiomama. As well as designing for Habitat, Lexon and Giannini, she also works on more personal projects under the Studiomama name. In *Pallet Project*, she demonstrated the principles of 'self-sufficiency, reusability, accessibility, utility and metamorphosis' with a collection of furniture, objects and lamps made from used pallets. Tolstrup described this project as 'durable, accessible and an agent for social change'.

Tostrup started out in 2006 with the *10, Ten, X project*, for which she designed a few pieces. An exhibition of this furniture attracted so much interest that she decided to publish the instructions for making some of the furniture and lamps on her website. The project went global, while retaining 'the idea of using a local resource, the pallet'. Since then, thousands of pieces of furniture in the Studiomama spirit have sprung up throughout the world.

In Argentina, some of these chairs, customized by great names in the design world, have been auctioned to raise funds for a charity project in Buenos Aires. Presided over by the photographer and gallerist Cecilia Glik, *Amistad o Nada* offers work to unemployed people, who use plans by Nina Tolstrup to make chairs from pallets and sell them. The profits are used to set up other workshops in the shanty towns, so providing a source of income to the most disadvantaged.

Studiomama

21-23 Voss Street - E2 6JE London, UK - Tel: +44 (0)207 033 0408
tolstrup@studiomama.com - www.studiomama.com

1. *Pallet Chandelier* ▪ 2. *Pallet Stool* ▪ 3. *1 X 1 Bookends* ▪ 4. Conference table ▪ 5. *Pallet Floor Lamp*
6. *Pollocky* chair by Gavin Turk ▪ 7. *Block Stool Blue & Block Stool Red* ▪ 8. *1 X 1 Table Lamp*
9. *Pallet Chair High* ▪ 10. Conference table chairs by Benchmark

CINCHAS SUN LOUNGER

Descended from the 'deck chairs' that graced the decks of transatlantic steamers before percolating down to suburban gardens, sun loungers have become a symbol *par excellence* of chilling out, lotus-eating and *dolce far niente*. This pallet interpretation of a great design classic is by M&M Designers.

Cinchas (Spanish for 'strap') was the name hit upon by Martin for this unique creation when it was still at the design stage. And it stuck.

DESIGN:
M&M DESIGNERS

CINCHAS SUN LOUNGER

TOOLBOX

Tools

- Tools
- Handsaw
- Jigsaw
- Screw gun
- Orbital sander

Materials

- 2 double-wing stringer pallets (used here: 950 (3'1½") x 1150mm (3'9¼")/7-board top deck/5-board bottom deck)
- Double-threaded wood screws for the outside
- 4 ratchet straps
- 4 100 (4") x 100mm (4") zinc-coated steel hinges

Telling details: Ratchet straps are an original touch.
The lounger folds for easy storage.

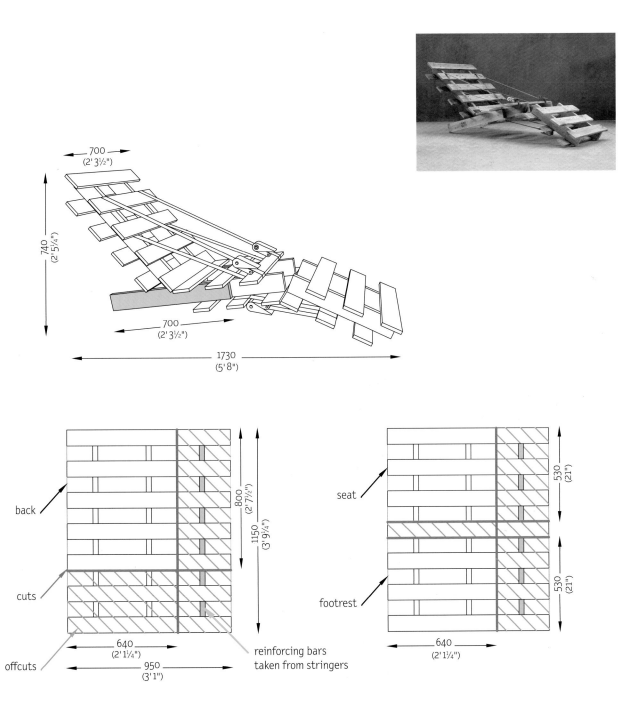

700
(2' 3½")

740
(2' 5¼")

700
(2' 3½")

1730
(5' 8")

back

cuts

offcuts

640
(2' 1¼")

950
(3' 1")

800
(2' 7½")

1150
(3' 9¼")

reinforcing bars
taken from stringers

seat

footrest

640
(2' 1¼")

530
(21")

530
(21")

All measurements are given in millimetres and inches (to nearest fraction)

Method

1. Cut both pallets to the dimensions shown on the plan. You will then have the 3 sections making up the sun lounger: the back, seat and footrest. Use the jigsaw for the boards and the handsaw for the stringers, which are thicker and harder to reach. Sand.

2. Using 2 of the hinges, assemble the back and seat. Repeat, using remaining hinges, for the seat and footrest.

3. Salvage the stringers from the offcuts and cut 2 700mm (2'3½") lengths to make the protuding feet of the lounger.

4. Position each bar overlapping 250mm (9¾") of the stringers making up the seat, leaving a 450mm (17¾") overhang for the feet.

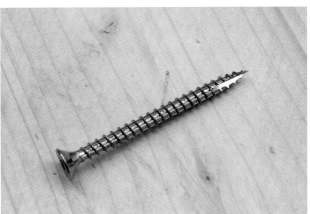

5. Clamp the stringers in position, then screw in the screws in a staggered line.

6. <u>Tip</u>: In order to avoid the risk of splitting the wood with classic wood screws, drill pilot holes of a smaller diameter than your screws. You can also use special rifled shank wood screws designed to reduce splitting.

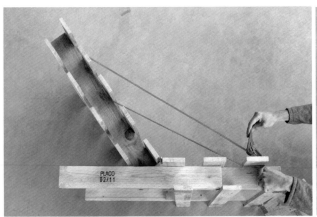

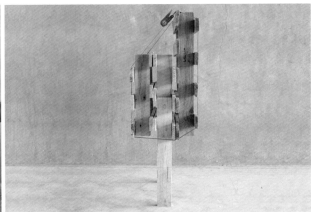

7. Fit the ratchet straps between the back and the seat (as shown). Regulate the tension to obtain the desired angle. Repeat with the straps between the seat and the footrest.

8. Hinged, so it folds up and is held neatly in place by the straps, the lounger requires little storage space.

M&M Designers
Martin Lévêque and Mathieu Maingourd

M&M Designers are a talented Franco-Belgian design duo. Each of these young designers has his own practice, but they get together regularly to work on shared projects. Both agree that 'design is a mixture of art, technique and humanity'. They don't have favourite materials, but they share the same concern: that their designs should carry the message that 'the concept is narrated by the object'.

How did you start designing furniture from wooden pallets?
Martin: The pallet has left its own environment behind in order to enter daily life; this is a highly creative approach. An approach that asks, how can you take a pallet apart and put it back together in order to give it a practical use? The answers are many and broad-ranging, from rigorous pieces such as dining tables to modular pieces such as shelves and adjustable pieces such as the sun lounger.

Mathieu: Pallet furniture isn't new, nor is the DIY approach. Designers interpret existing materials. We have interpreted pallets in line with our respective cultures and personalities.

What inspires your designs?
Martin: Our aim was to offer furniture that was easy to make and simple to use, with shapes that were easy to read. Hijacked from its original purpose, the pallet was in itself an inspiration for original furniture.

Mathieu: We haven't created new pieces of furniture, we have interpreted existing ones. The salvage process itself gives meaning to the material. In a pallet you see lines, but how can you design a piece of furniture in which you see only that? The *Lineup* dining table was the beginning of an answer to this question.

What are the pros and cons of working with pallets?
Martin: The weight is a constraint that you have to take into consideration, as they make heavy furniture. And as far as comfort goes you have to find a compromise, especially for chairs.

Mathieu: The pallet offers real freedom. And when you do it yourself, your involvement is greater. There is great deal of increased value in this act of creation.

Martin Lévêque
44, rue Eeckelaers - 1210 Brussels, Belgium
kadiak29@hotmail.com
http://be.net/martinleveque

Mathieu Maingourd
13, rue Barbe-Torte - 44200 Nantes, France
math_ology@hotmail.com
http://dopirate.free.fr

INVADER
COFFEE TABLE

No living room is complete without its coffee table – practical, naturally, but also an integral part of the decorative scheme. Serving by turns as a children's desk, an exhibition space for showing off our favourite ornaments and a handy surface for drinks and nibbles with friends, it plays a central part in our lives. A role that this *Invader* table takes on with panache.

Making a virtue of its notched stringers and adding endearing little legs, this coffee table has the irresistible look of one of the *Space Invaders* that gave it its name.

DESIGN:
M&M DESIGNERS

INVADER COFFEE TABLE

TOOLBOX

Tools

- Drill (with ø9mm (²³⁄₆₄") wood bit)
- Handsaw
- Jigsaw
- Screw gun
- Orbital sander + sanding block
- Clamps
- 1 flat paintbrush
- 1 round paintbrush

Materials

- 2 notched stringer pallets (here 1060 (3'5¾") x 1110mm (3'7¾"))
- Double-threaded wood screws
- ø8mm (⁵⁄₁₆") Dowel pins
- 4 corner brackets (75 (3") x 75 (3") x 105mm (4"))
- Wood glue
- Coloured chalk
- Wood paint (white)

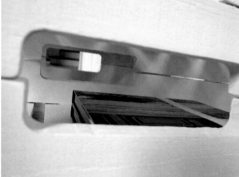

Telling details: Storage space under the top deck.
A nod in the direction of the well-known video game.

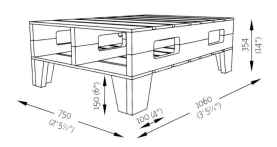

354
(14")

150 (6")

750
(2'5½")

100 (4")

1060
(3'5¾")

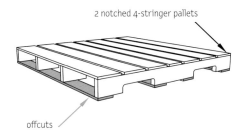

2 notched 4-stringer pallets

offcuts

4 legs from offcuts

90
(3½")

140
(5½")

150
(6")

50
(2")

100
(4")

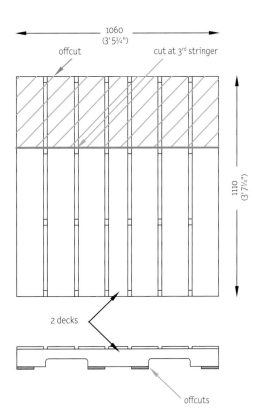

1060
(3'5¾")

offcut

cut at 3ʳᵈ stringer

1110
(3'7¾")

2 decks

offcuts

All measurements are given in millimetres and inches (to nearest fraction)

Method

1. Remove the bottom deckboards from both pallets. If the boards are not too thick, use a hammer to break them between the stringers, then remove the pieces by hand. (Otherwise use method 3, p.16.)

2. Shear off the nails left in the stringers with an angle grinder, grinding them down until they are flush with the wood. Wear safety spectacles, gloves and ear defenders, and be careful not to mark the wood by bringing the angle grinder too close to the surface.

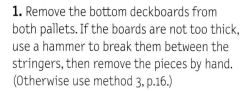

3. Use a rule to draw a cutting line along the third stringer, slightly to the side so that the jigsaw does not hit the stringer as you cut.

4. Saw along the line, keeping the offcuts to make the table legs.

5. Using an orbital sander, sand both decks, starting with coarse sandpaper and finishing with fine. For the top deck forming the table top, use a sanding block to round off the edges of the boards.

6. Assemble the two decks using dowel pins. Mark the positions of the 6 pins accurately on the stringers of one of the pallets. Using a 9mm diameter wood drill bit, drill holes approximately 2mm (1/16") deeper than the pins in order to leave room for the glue.

7. Insert the dowel pins, then cover them liberally with chalk in order to mark out the second deck.

8. Place the second deck carefully over the dowel pins, then press down to mark their positions.

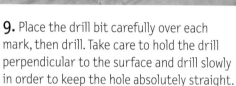

9. Place the drill bit carefully over each mark, then drill. Take care to hold the drill perpendicular to the surface and drill slowly in order to keep the hole absolutely straight.

10. Check that the two decks fit together properly, then squeeze wood glue into each dowel hole to strengthen the hold.

11. To make painting easier, do it before you finally fit the two decks together. Paint a first coat, let it dry, then sand lightly with fine glass paper before applying the second.

12. From the offcuts, salvage 8 lengths of wood of at least 300mm (11¾") to make the legs. Make 4 pairs and glue them together with wood glue, securing them with clamps until they dry.

13. Mark out the shape of the legs, following the plans, to give 4 smaller pieces (50 (2") x 150 (6") x 90mm (3½")) and 4 larger ones (140 (5½") x 150 (6") x 100mm (4")). Saw, sand and paint the legs.

14. For each leg, join a smaller and larger piece together using a corner bracket.

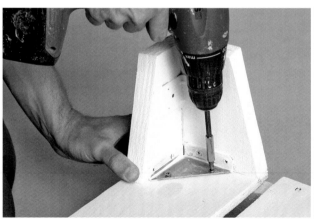

15. Screw on the legs, taking care to ensure that the wider parts appear on the long sides of the table, where they will match the width of the deckboards.

16. To finish off your table, you can, if you wish, add a glass top. Ask a professional to cut a piece of glass to fit, at least 6mm (¼") thick and with polished edges.

THEATRE BEAD HEAD

To customize your bedroom with dramatic flair, look no further than this original headboard. With its built-in niches and lamps, it is also highly practical. Designed here for a bed 160cm (5'3") wide, it can easily be adapted to suit your own beds.

Like the backdrop to a stage production, the *Theatre* bed head makes a statement. Its lighting is practical for reading in bed while also setting off the contents of the niches and contributing to an atmospheric lighting scheme for the room as a whole. Like stage lighting, it performs multiple functions, lending clarity and visibility, creating an ambience and focusing attention on specific objects.

DESIGN:
LE FOURBI CRÉATIF DE MACHA

THEATRE **BEAD HEAD**

TOOLBOX

Tools

- Jigsaw
- Orbital sander
- Screw gun
- Hammer
- 1 small round paintbrush
- 1 flat paintbrush
- 1 round paintbrush

Materials

- 2 1000 (3'3½") x 1200mm (3'11¼") reversible stringer pallets
- 1 pallet with 140mm (5½")-wide boards
- Double-threaded wood screws
- Round-head nails, 25mm (1") long
- 5 jointing plates, 80 (3¼") x 40mm (1½")
- 2 wing nuts
- For the lamps: 2 sockets, 2 rocker switches, 1 4m (13') length white fabric-covered lighting flex, 2 plugs, 2 bulbs
- Wood paint in the colour of your choice

Telling details: Handy niches built into the bedhead.
The lamps shed a light that is at once filtered and functional.

1020
(3'4¼")

2400
(7'10½")

2 reversible stringer pallets

1200
(3'11¼")

1000
(3'3½")

pallet with 140mm (5½")-wide boards

1200
(3'11¼")

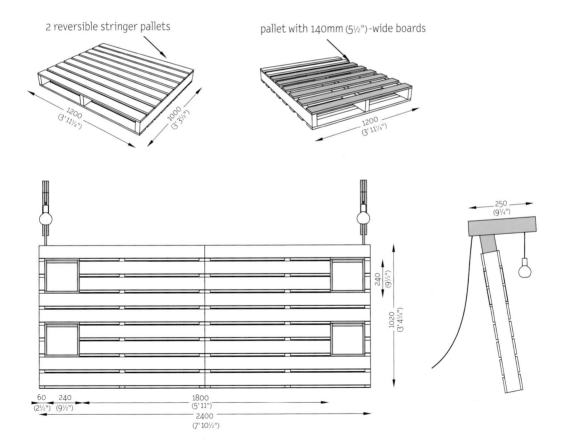

240
(9½")

1020
(3'4¼")

250
(9¾")

60
(2½")

240
(9½")

1800
(5'11")

2400
(7'10½")

All measurements are given in millimetres and inches (to nearest fraction)

Method

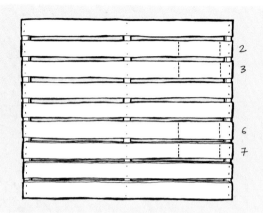

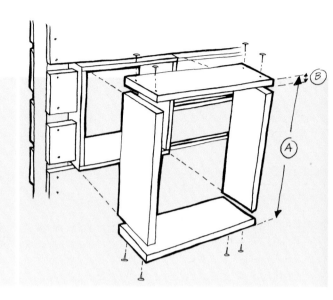

1. On each pallet, cut out boards 2, 3, 6 and 7 60mm (2½") in from the end and to a width of 240mm (9½") in order to make the holes for the niches. Sand the pallets, taking special care to obtain a perfectly smooth finish.

2. To make the niches, use boards that are wider than those of your pallets so that they stand proud. Cut 8 lengths of 240mm (9½"), plus 8 more corresponding to the height of the niches (height = A−(2 x B)). Assemble the niches using round-head nails. Nail them into the pallets to the depth of the boards.

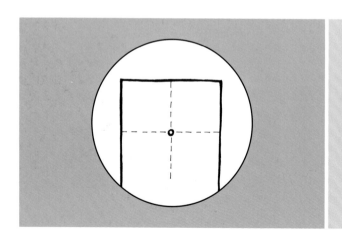

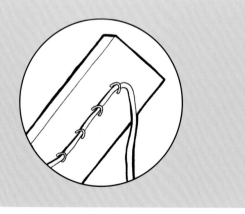

3. To make the lamps, cut out and sand 6 boards of 250mm (9¾"). Mark a point at the centre of each board's width and the same distance from the end, and drill a hole of the same diameter as your wing nuts.

4. Using cable clips, attach the flex to one of the boards making up the articulated arm of the lamp. Take care to measure the length of the drop against the height of your bed, so that the lamps do not hang too high or too low.

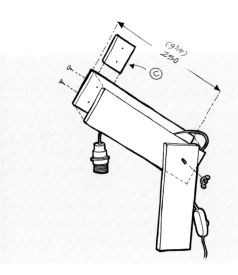

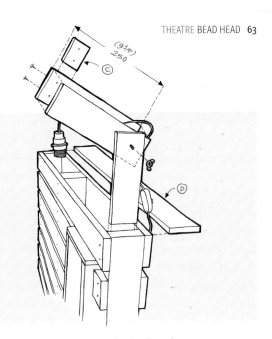

5. Assemble the 3 boards for each lamp with the wing nuts. Using glue and nails, attach a piece of wood measuring 20mm (¾") (C on the plan, cut from an offcut) to the end of the articulated arm.

6. Screw the lamp on to the bedhead. To finish, cut, sand and nail boards (D) to cover the top of the pallets.
Safety warning: *follow the instructions with that came with your appliance*; if in doubt, consult a professional.

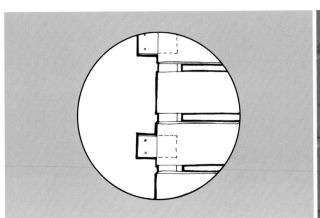

7. Join the 2 pallet together using 5 80 (3¼") x 40mm (1½") jointing plates.

8. In its masculine livery of neutral brown shades, the bed head adds a note of classic elegance to the bedroom.

Fabrice Peltier
P'Référence agency

Fabrice Peltier in 6 dates

1961: Born in Paris.

1985: Sets up the design agency P'Référence.

2003: Foundation of the Institut National du Design Packaging.

2007: *Ecodesign, chemins vertueux* published by Editions Pyramyd.

2008: Opening of the Designpack Gallery.

2011: Opening of the Allée de Recyclage.

Packaging designer and founder of the P'Référence agency, Fabrice Peltier is an enthusiastic proponent of eco-design, with an approach aimed at designing products that respect the environment throughout their life cycle. 'Once it is emptied of its contents, packaging should not be considered merely as rubbish, but should instead be viewed as the raw material for recycling or transforming.' Exhibitions of his work illustrate this principle with designs based on recycled packaging, pallets and other everyday items, offering clever and playful alternatives to passive consumerism.

At his *Made in Palette* show, held in November 2010 at the Designpack Gallery, Fabrice Peltier posed questions as to the future that lies in store for pallets when they reach the end of their useful lives. What is to be done with a pallet that can't be put back into circulation? His response took the form of a collection of furniture and lamps made entirely from used pallets (all produced by Ateliers Services in Lisieux, a project aimed at achieving social integration through economic activity).

Once dismantled, the blocks and boards of old pallets are assembled according to the same principle for every piece: the blocks are glued together to form the framework, and the boards are then sawn up and nailed directly on to this structure.

Some of Peltier's pieces may be seen in the 'Allée de Recyclage', a new permanent exhibition space in the corridors of the Paris Métro, at the Palais-Royal—Musée du Louvre station – a unique exhibition space in which to discover 'a panorama of art from throughout the world and a way of transforming discarded packaging into new and useful (or useless) objects'.

Designpack Gallery
24, rue de Richelieu - 75001 Paris, France - Tel: +1 44 85 86 00
gallery@p-reference.fr - www.p-reference.fr/www.designpackgallery.fr

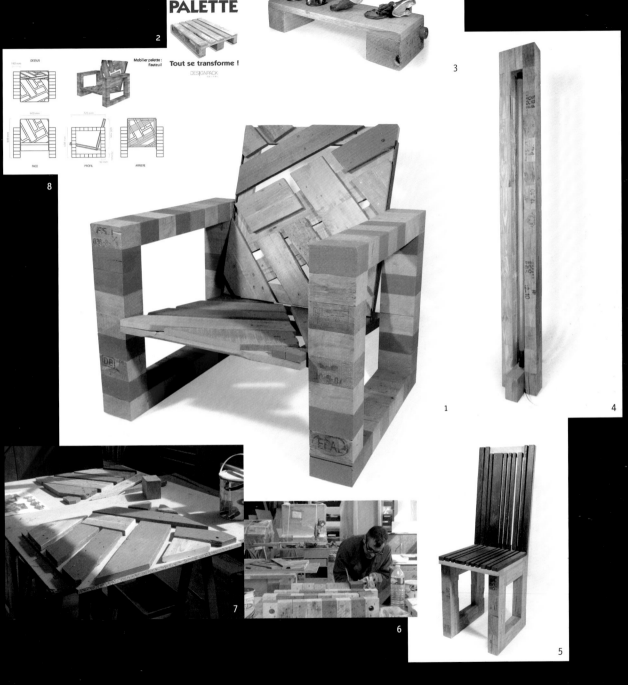

1. *Vrac* Armchair. ▪ 2. Exhibition poster for *Made in Palette* ▪ 3. *Décomposition.* ▪ 4. *Néon* large pillar.
5. *Code barre* Chair. ▪ 6. Making a *Vrac* armchair at Ateliers Services.
7. Painting the parts of a *Vrac* armchair ▪ 8. Manufacturing plans for a *Vrac* armchair

WHERE IS BRIAN?
COAT STAND

Banished from contemporary hallways for many years, the old-fashioned coat stand is long overdue a revival. Gradually, thanks to the imagination of innovative designers, the idea is being dusted off and rethought in fresh materials and new shapes. The *Where is Brian?* coat stand, brainchild of Mr&Mlle™, offers a practical solution to the perennial problem of where to hang those jackets, hats and bags.

Where is Brian? is a reference to the hero of French school textbooks that will raise a wry smile among all those who have been at the teaching or receiving end of English lessons in France. Follow the arrow to discover – along with cohorts of French schoolchildren – that 'Brian is in the kitchen!'.

DESIGN:
MR&MLLE™

WHERE IS BRIAN? COAT STAND

TOOLBOX	
Tools	**Materials**
▪ Jigsaw	▪ 1 950 (3'1½") x 1150mm (3'9¼") stringer pallet (here the boards measure 90 (3½") x 1150 (3'9¼") x 20mm (¾") and the stringers 90 (3½") x 950 (3'1½") x 35mm (1⅜"))
▪ Handsaw	
▪ Mitre box	
▪ Hacksaw	
▪ Chisel	▪ Wood screws
▪ Screw gun	▪ Countersunk wood screws
▪ Orbital sander	▪ Stencils for words or letters (or make your own using computer and printer) + scalpel
▪ Clamps	
▪ Metal square	▪ Repositionable spray adhesive
▪ 1 small foam paint roller	▪ Wood paint in the colours of your choice
▪ 1 very fine round paintbrush	

Telling details: The pegs double as signs.
Pop-art colours add to the cartoon feel.

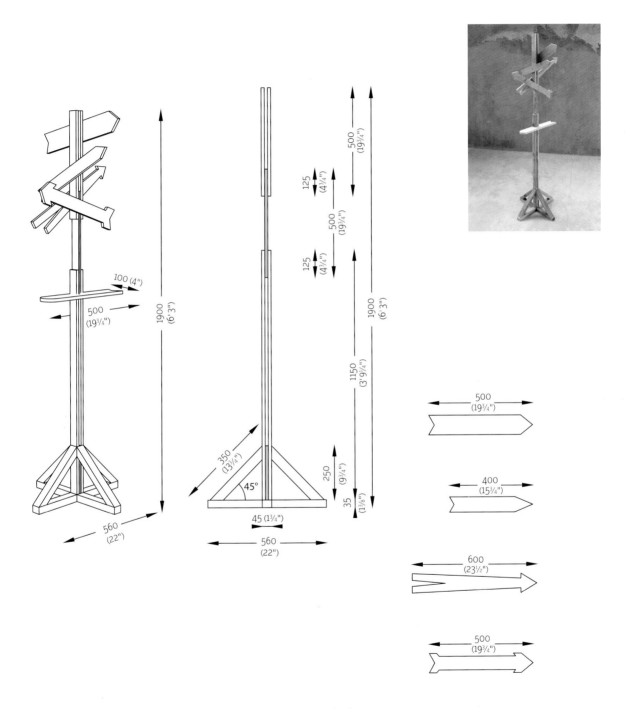

100 (4")

500
(19¾")

1900
(6'3")

560
(22")

500
(19¾")

125
(4¾")

500
(19¾")

125
(4¾")

1900
(6'3")

1150
(3'9¾")

350
(13¾")

45°

45 (1¾")

560
(22")

250
(9¾")

35
(1⅜")

500
(19¾")

400
(15¾")

600
(23½")

500
(19¾")

All measurements are given in millimetres and inches (to nearest fraction)

Method

1. Dismantle the pallet following method 3, p.16, in order to salvage 5 deckboards and 2 stringers.

2. To make the shaft of the stand, use the jigsaw to cut 2 of the boards in half lengthways, to obtain 4 pieces measuring 45 (1¾") x 1150mm (3'9¼").

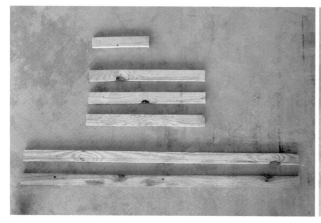

3. Set aside 2 1150mm (3'9¼") lengths of board. Saw the 2 remaining boards as follows: 2 500mm (19¾") lengths from the first board; 1 500mm (19¾") length and 1 250mm (9¾") length from the second. Sand all these pieces.

4. To assemble the shaft, first screw the 250mm (9¾") length, flush at the end, between the 2 1150mm (3'9¼") lengths.

5. Attach one of the 500mm (19¾") lengths to the other end of the shaft, overlapping the boards by 125mm (4¾"). Refer to the plan to position each piece.

6. Finish off the shaft by screwing the last two 500mm (19¾") lengths to either side of the 500mm (19¾") length in the previous step, again overlapping by 125mm (4¾"). Take care to keep the pieces straight and flush as you work.

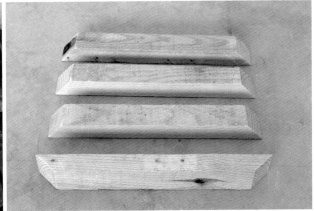

7. For the base, use the jigsaw to saw the stringers in half lengthways, to obtain 4 pieces measuring 45 (1¾") x 950mm (3'1½"). Saw them again to obtain 4 350mm (13¾") lengths and 2 560mm (22") lengths.

8. Using the jigsaw and mitre box, saw the ends of the 4 350mm (13¾") lengths at an angle of 45 degrees. Sand.

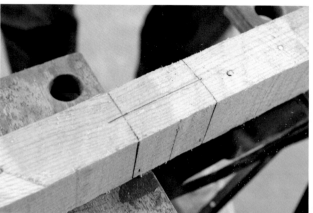

9. Make a half-joint to form the cross of the base. Mark the centre of the two pieces of 560mm (22") length, then place them on top of each other at right angles. Mark the width of the upper stringer on the lower one and vice versa.

10. Using a square, extend the lines round the sides, then join them with a central horizontal line.

11. Use the jigsaw to cut notches in the stringers up to the central line.

12. Finish the cut with the chisel.

13. Check for fit, then screw the cross pieces together.

14. Screw the cross shape to the shaft.

15. Countersink the ends of the 4 350mm (13¾") lengths, so that the screws lie flush with the wood.

16. Screw the 4 pieces to the shaft and the cross.

17. From one of the remaining boards, cut a 500mm (19¾") length to make the shelf built into the shaft. You can make it any shape you like.

18. Mark the centre line of the board. Transfer the dimensions of the lower part of the shaft to the middle of the shelf, in order to mark out the notches (3 times the width of the boards forming the shaft.) Saw out the notches, then sand the board.

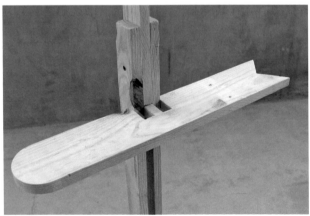

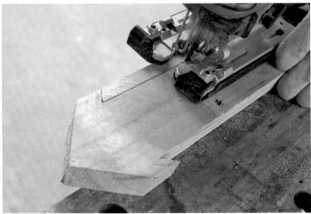

19. Insert the board into the lower part of the shaft, using a spirit level to make sure it is horizontal.

20. Use the remaining boards to mark out, and cut, arrows to serve as pegs.

21. Screw the arrows to the shaft, playing around with their positions until you find a layout you like.

22. If you are making your own stencils, use word-processing software, choosing the typeface and size for the indications you want to give (rooms in the house, distance to nearby towns, different countries, etc.), then print them on thick paper (no less than 120gsm).
Cut them out carefully with a scalpel.

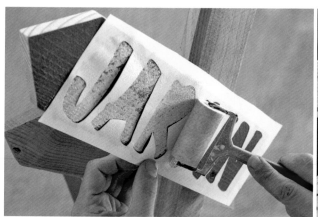

23. For best results, spray the back of the stencil (whether bought or home-made) with the repositionable adhesive and leave it until it starts to 'take'. Put the stencil in place, then gently apply the paint with a small foam roller.

24. Alternate the colours you use for the letters and backgrounds, while always letting the wood show through.

MISS TABLE
GARDEN TABLE

Designed for outside use, the *Miss Table* picnic table can be dismantled for easy storage. The principle by which the legs are set in beneath the top is as simple as a child's construction toy – so this design is not only a marriage of elegance and practicality but is also quick and easy to assemble.

The table is named in homage to Miss Marple, Agatha Christie's much-loved amateur lady detective, famous for slotting the pieces of murder mysteries together over a pot of tea and a genteel tea table.

DESIGN:
PHILIPPE DANEY

MISS TABLE **GARDEN TABLE**

TOOLBOX	
Tools	**Materials**
▪ Handsaw	▪ 1 800 (2'7½") x 1200mm (3'11¼") Euro pallet (or 1 9-block solid pallet)
▪ Orbital sander	▪ 1 800 (2'7½") x 1200mm (3'11¼") pallet, if possible, with boards of different lengths and thicknesses
▪ Screw gun	
▪ Clamps	
▪ 1 small paint roller	▪ Double-threaded wood screws
▪ 1 fine round brush	▪ Exterior wood paint in the colour of your choice

Telling details: The legs slot under the top for easy assembly.
The design combines practicality with elegance.

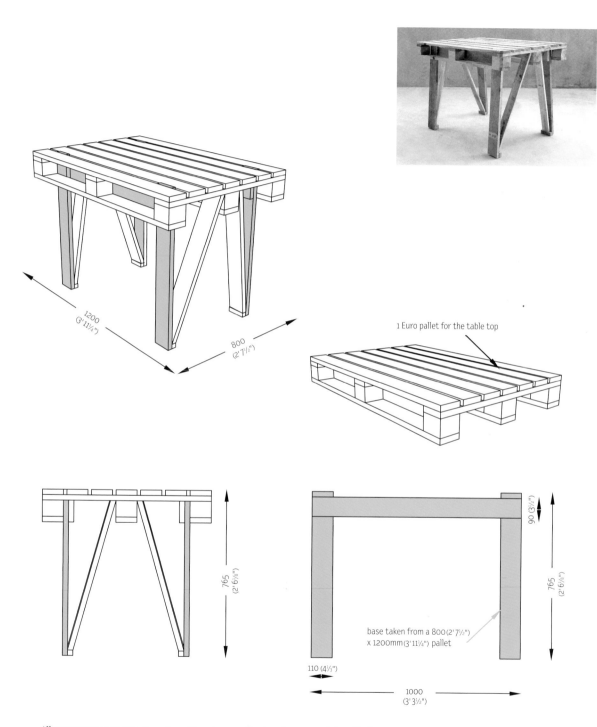

1200
(3'11¼")

800
(2'7½")

1 Euro pallet for the table top

765
(2'6⅛")

90 (3½")

765
(2'6⅛")

base taken from a 800 (2'7½")
x 1200mm (3'11¼") pallet

110 (4⅓")

1000
(3'3½")

All measurements are given in millimetres and inches (to nearest fraction)

Method

1. Dismantle the 800 (2'7½") x 1200mm (3'11¼") pallet following method 1, p.16. Salvage 10 boards to make the table base: 6 for the two U-shaped pieces and 4 for the struts.

2. Place the block pallet to be used for the top upside-down on the ground. To decide the height of the legs, slot one of the salvaged boards in the space between the first two boards of the deck.

3. Draw a cutting line at the height decided (here 750mm (2'5½")). Saw. Now you have the template for the three other legs.

4. For the length of the side brace, wedge the end of the board flush with the block of the deck, then make a mark on a line with the block at the other end. Saw.

5. Position the legs and the side brace on the under side of the deck/top, holding them in place with clamps.

6. Screw the side brace to the legs, making sure that the boards serving as legs have their sawn ends on the ground when the table is turned the right way up.

7. Repeat to make the second U-shape. These are made with the 6 thickest boards (25mm (1") thick by 110mm (4⅓") wide).

8. The 4 remaining boards will serve as struts to brace the table legs and give them greater stability. To determine the length of the struts, wedge one of these boards between the block of the deck/top and the leg, then draw a line at the bottom of the board.

9. Mark out the top of the board. Saw. Repeat with the 3 other boards.

10. A wedge will be needed to hold the strut against the leg. To determine the wedge height, position the strut against the leg (pushing the leg backwards slightly in order to ensure a tight fit when you insert the strut in step 13), then draw a mark.

11. Place an offcut against this mark to transfer the dimension. Mark your cutting line, then saw to make the wedges. Repeat for the other 3 wedges.

12. Screw the wedges to the ends of the legs.

13. Insert the struts. The pallet used provides boards of two different thicknesses and widths; the boards used here for the struts are thus thinner (15mm (½")) and narrower (75mm (3")) in order to reduce the weight of the base. But you can also use boards that are the same as for the U-shaped pieces.

14. Sand the table with coarse sandpaper in order to remove any risk of splinters. Do not try to make the surface completely smooth, however, the idea being to retain a slightly uneven finish suitable for outdoor furniture.

15. Choose an exterior wood paint to protect your table from the elements. Use a small roller to paint the boards of the top and a fine round brush for the base.

Philippe Daney
Designer-architect

Philippe in 6 dates

1956: Born in Neuilly-sur-Seine, France.

1986: Organizes the art event '*La Nuit de l'Ange*'.

1995: Meets Michel Roset.

1997: Théâtre National de Rennes, France, *Le Voyage d'Urien*, based on a text by André Gide.

2002: Sets up the Daney Factory in the centre of Rennes, France.

2008: Exhibition at the Musée d'Art Moderne Richard Anacréon, Granville, France. Appointed a Chevalier des Arts et des Lettres.

An architect by training, Philippe Daney is also by turns a designer, publisher, theatre director and artist. In parallel with his work as a designer for publishers such as Cinna and Ligne Roset, he designs lighting schemes for private and public spaces and teaches his skills at a college of applied arts. 'I have been a teacher for twenty-three years, passing on knowledge is an integral part of who I am. That is the chief virtue of this book: designing to share. And saying: 'Now you can do it too!'

What inspires your designs?

For my lamps, the starting point was broken pallets and offcuts. I've always enjoyed working with scrap, because this lends greater integrity to the idea of salvage, taking it to its logical conclusion. You use a pallet because it is damaged and discarded, and will never be used again. I like the ambiguity of the *The Shadow's Share No 2* lamp. What is it exactly, a wall lamp or a floor lamp? It is an object that gains life and meaning both from its materials and from its plays of light and shadow.

How did you start designing furniture from wooden pallets?

Working with pallets is interesting both for the material of which they are made, wood, and also for their intrinsic quality, the relationship between solid and empty space that defines them. My idea was to design furniture that would respect the rhythm of the pallet.

What are the pros and cons of working with pallets?

Pallets possess a strong aesthetic — the industrial aesthetic of raw wood and a form dictated by the strength of its lines. They are tough, and even if they have a few damaged boards they are easy to repair. But you have to make sure they are properly dry. If a pallet is still even slightly damp when you bring it inside, you run the risk of it splitting under the effects of heat.

What advice would you give to someone starting out as a designer of furniture and objects from pallets?

This is a raw material that allows you to react instantly and with perfect freedom, since you can simply start again if it goes wrong; that's the nature of salvage. It takes the stress out of the design process, and also out of the colours you choose — after all, painting wood is no big deal!

Daney Factory

13, rue de Bray - 35777 Cesson-Sévigné, France - Tel: +2 99 14 36 99
collectif@agence-daney.com - www.philippedaney.com

  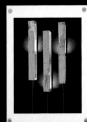  

Left to right: *Man's Best Friend* floor lamp (p.26) ▪ *Miss Table* garden table (p.76) ▪ *Peace and Light* wall lights (p.116)
The Suitcase floor lamp (p.142) ▪ *The Shadow's Share №2* standard lamp (p.174)

MICHEL
DESK

For the designers of this desk, the objective was to retain the identity of the pallet. How to design a desk with light, airy lines while at the same time keeping the outlines of a wooden pallet? Simple to assemble, its construction lightened by the use of smoked glass, the *Michel* desk is the answer, transforming a pallet into a piece of stylish contemporary furniture.

Mr&Mlle are therefore proud to introduce their new baby, *Michel* – a knowing wink in the direction of those for whom a desk is an altogether more serious and pretentious affair.

DESIGN:
MR&MLLE™

MICHEL DESK

TOOLBOX

Tools

- Drill (with ø16mm (⅝") wood bit)
- Handsaw
- Hacksaw
- Screw gun
- Orbital sander and sanding block
- 1 large flat paintbrush
- 1 small round paintbrush

Materials

- 2 1000 (3'3½") x 1200mm (3'11¼") reversible stringer pallets, with 8 boards to each deck
- 2 1200mm (3'11¼")-long deckboards (varying in width according to your pallet)
- 2m (6'6") of varnished steel tubing (ø16mm (⅝"))
- 2 500 (19¾") x 300mm (11¾") zinc-coated steel hinges
- 6 30 (1¼") x 30mm (1¼") square-ended angle braces
- Wood paint in the colour of your choice
- 1 800 (2'7½") x 400mm (15¾") sheet of smoked glass

Telling details: A hidden compartment for files and stationery.
Extra storage space under the worktop.

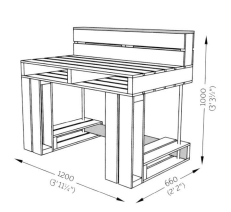

1200
(3'11¼")

660
(2'2")

1000
(3'3½")

reversible stringer pallet
for the top

cuts

1000
(3'3½")

1200
(3'11¼")

reversible stringer pallet
for the legs

offcuts

cuts

1200
(3'11¼")

1000
(3'3½")

boards for the desk top and bottom strut
taken from a 1200mm (3'11¼")pallet

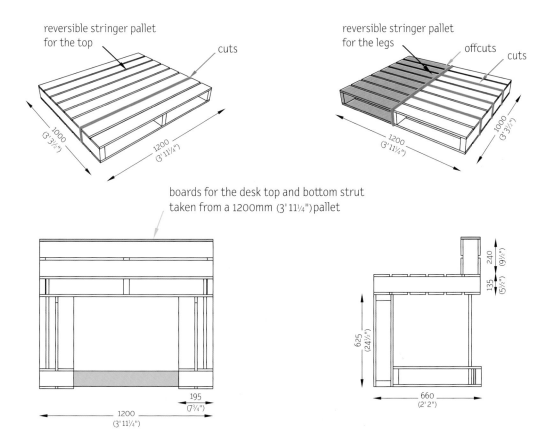

195
(7¾")

1200
(3'11¼")

240
(9½")

135
(5½")

625
(24½")

660
(2'2")

All measurements are given in millimetres and inches (to nearest fraction)

Method

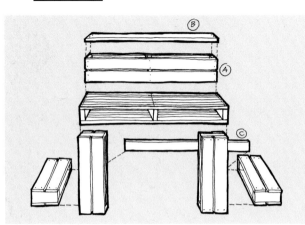

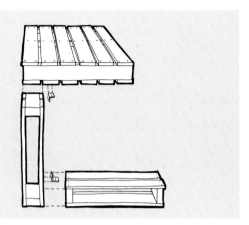

1. Cut all the sections of the desk according to the plans, taking the 4 base sections (195 (7¾") x 625mm (24½")) from one, and the desk top and back extension from the second. Sand carefully to obtain a smooth surface. Roughly sand the interiors with the sanding block.

2. Stand one base section on the ground, then place a second perpendicular to it to form the 'L' of the legs. Assemble them, and the top, using angle braces.

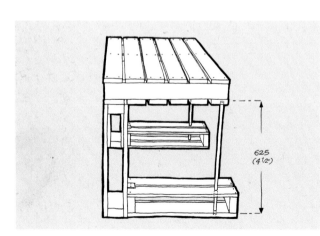

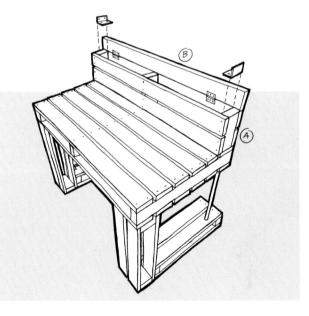

3. Cut 2 625mm (24½") lengths of steel tubing (to match the height of the legs). Check the position of the tube, then, with a ø16mm (⅝") wood bit, drill a hole through the first board of the leg and halfway through the second. Drill halfway through the top board, then insert the tube. Repeat on the other side.

4. Attach the back extension (A) to the desk top with angle braces. Make a cover for the top with a board (B) and two hinges.

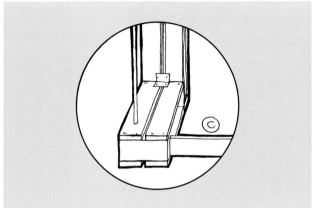

5. For the bottom strut (C), screw a board to the legs at both ends.

6. Paint the desk, highlighting its lines by picking out only a few of the boards. The combination of black and untreated wood gives the desk a classic look with a contemporary twist.

7. In a simplified version of the traditional hidden drawer found in so many antique desks, the *Michel* desk has its own concealed (if not exactly secret) compartment to add extra, semi-private storage space.

8. The gap between the pallet's top and bottom decks provides more storage space to keep the desk top free of clutter.

GRAND LARGE
CORNER SHELF

At first glance you would never know this piece was made from pallet boards. Only when you look closely can you make out a few clues as to its origins. The *Grand Large* shelf is an exercise in the adaptability of the humble pallet. As its designer points out, with pallets 'you can embark on the most complicated creations without worrying about getting it wrong and ruining a piece of precious wood'. So let your imagination run wild.

The name (the French for 'deep wide ocean') is a metaphorical nod in the direction of the generous dimensions of the piece and of the designer's love for the rugged Breton coast. What better room for this, then, than the bathroom?

DESIGN:
BÉA

GRAND LARGE **CORNER SHELF**

TOOLBOX

Tools

- Hammer
- Hacksaw
- Jigsaw
- Screw gun
- Orbital sander
- 2 flat paintbrushes
- 1 small round paintbrush

Materials

- 1 reversible stringer pallet 900mm (2'11½") wide (with 7 boards on each side), or 2 single- or double-deck stringer pallets 900mm (2'11½") wide (with 7 boards on top)
- Double-threaded wood screws
- Dowel pins
- Wood glue
- 4 80 (3¼") x 10mm (⁷⁄₁₆") zinc-coated steel jointing plates
- 2 lenths (approx. 1.5m (5')) of 20mm (¾") baton
- Colourless matt bathroom varnish
- Wood paint in the colour of your choice

Telling details: A well-crafted piece for your bathroom.
The deep shelves offer generous and easy-to-reach storage space.

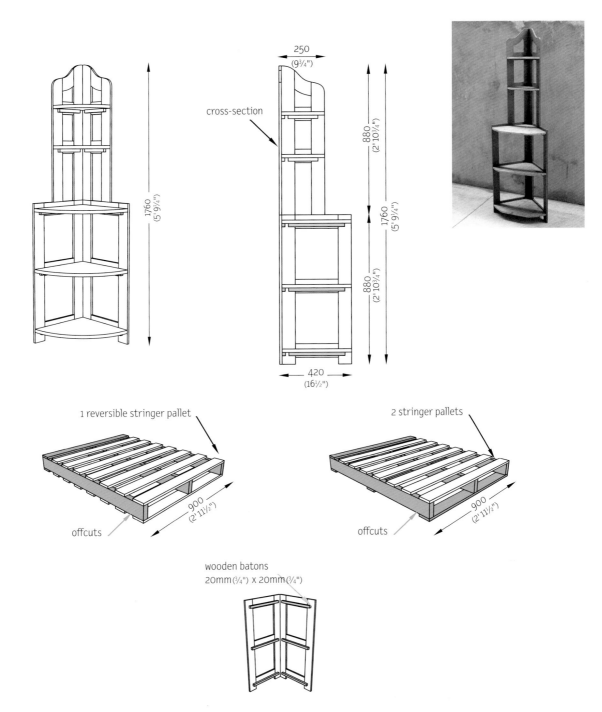

250
(9¾")

cross-section

880
(2'10¾")

1760
(5'9¼")

1760
(5'9¼")

880
(2'10¾")

420
(16½")

1 reversible stringer pallet

2 stringer pallets

900
(2'11½")

900
(2'11½")

offcuts

offcuts

wooden batons
20mm (¾") x 20mm (¾")

All measurements are given in millimetres and inches (to nearest fraction)

Method

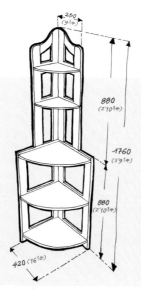

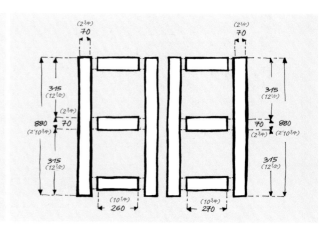

1. Dismantle the pallets according to method 3, p.16, in order to salvage 14 boards (here measuring 900 (2'11½") x 70 (2¾") x 15mm (½")). Sand all the boards with coarse sandpaper, then finish off with fine.

2. Cut up the boards according to the plan to make the uprights of the bottom section. Note that one upright has crosspieces of 260mm (10¼") and the other of 270mm (10¾"): as the uprights overlap when assembled, the thickness of the board has to be added to one side to ensure identical internal measurements.

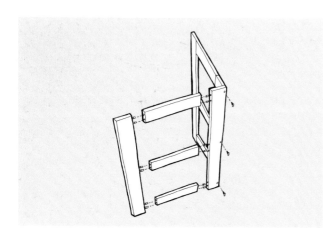

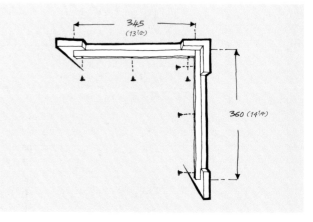

3. Assemble the parts of each upright using wood glue and dowel pins (see *Invader* coffee table, p.50). Then screw the two uprights together.

4. To support the shelves, screw lengths of 20mm (¾") baton to each upright, taking the dimensions from the plan above.

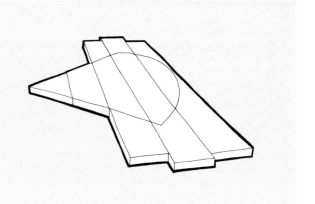

5. The bottom section is now ready to receive the shelves.

6. For the shelves, make a cardboard template in the form of a quarter circle with a radius of 395mm (15½"). Align 5 planks and use the template to mark out the shape of the shelf. Saw carefully and place the pieces on the support batons to check for fit.

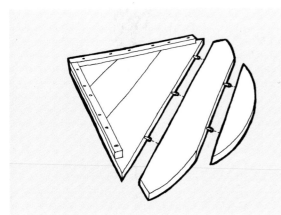

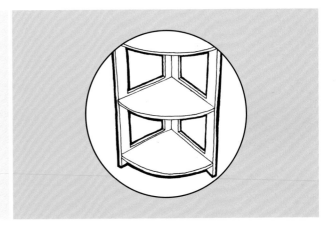

7. Use the support batons from the frame to make it easier to assemble the shelves. Place them on the shelves and fix them with glue and screws. For the outermost two boards, which cannot be attached to the wood strips, use glue and dowel pins.

8. Screw the support batons, with the shelves attached, to the uprights, in their original positions.

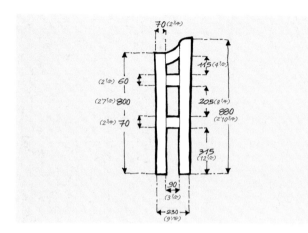

9. Cut out boards to make the top section, following the measurements on the plan.

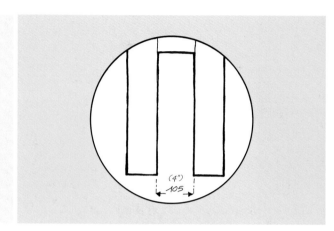

10. Note that, as with the bottom section, the crosspieces are of different lengths, in order to overlap: 90mm (3½") on one side and 105mm (4") on the other.

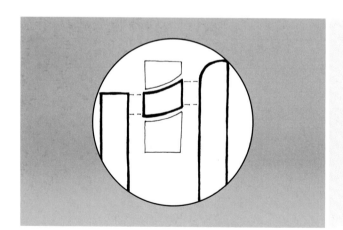

11. To make the template for the crosspiece, place the two uprights on a piece of paper, then place the board to be sawn on top of them, at an angle. Mark the outlines and draw in the curves. Transfer the pattern to the board. Saw. To assemble, follow step 4.

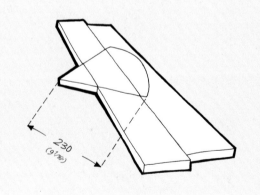

12. For the shelves, make a template of a quarter circle with a radius of 230mm (9¹⁄₁₆"). As for the bottom section, align the boards, transfer the outline and saw.

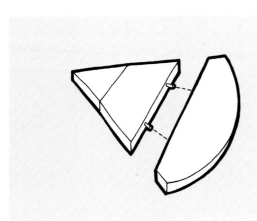

13. The shelves of the top section are assembled using only glue and dowel pins.

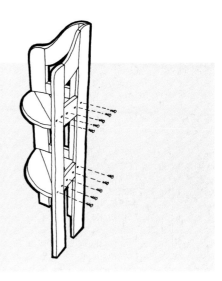

14. Screw the shelves to the uprights.

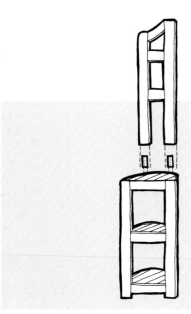

15. Assemble the top and bottom sections, using two jointing plates on each side.

16. Finish with bathroom varnish to protect against water and humidity.

UPHOLSTERER'S
POUFFE

Taking its name from the Arabic word for 'cushion', the pouffe is an omnipresent feature of oriental interiors that made its first appearance in Europe in the nineteenth century. With neither back nor armrests, it was perfectly suited to the age of the crinoline. Practical and easy to move around, handy as both a seat and a foot stool, it became as popular as it is useful. In this 'pallet' version, it also scores on the recycling front.

The name is a tribute to a traditional craft for which the designer, Marion Davaud, has a particular fondness. Here the webbing used by upholsterers as the seat framework is proudly on display.

DESIGN:
LE FOURBI CRÉATIF DE MACHA

UPHOLSTERER'S POUFFE

TOOLBOX	
Tools	**Materials**
■ Jigsaw ■ Drill (with ø9mm (²³⁄₆₄") wood bit) ■ Sheet sander ■ Hammer ■ Hacksaw ■ Clamps ■ Mitre saw ■ Flat paintbrush	■ 1 800 (2'7½") x 1200mm (3'11¼") double-deck stringer pallet (board dimensions here 100mm (4") (Width) x 20mm (¾")) ■ 1 800 (2'7½") x 1200mm (3'11¼") 9-block pallet (board dimensions here 80mm (3¼") (Width) x 15mm (½")/blocks 75 (3") x 75mm (3")) ■ Upholstery tacks (ø14mm (³⁵⁄₆₄")) ■ Nails (ø3 (⅛") x 70mm (2¾")/ø2.2 (⁵⁄₆₄") x 40mm (1½")) ■ Round-head nails (ø1.6 (¹⁄₁₆") x 30mm (1¼")) ■ 60mm (2½") jute webbing x 5m (16'4") ■ Wood glue ■ Dowel pins (ø8mm (⁵⁄₁₆")) ■ Wood paint in a colour of your choice

Telling details: A handy and easy-to-move form of extra seating.
The jute webbing adds comfort and style.

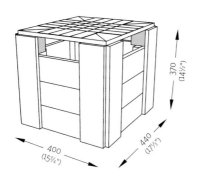

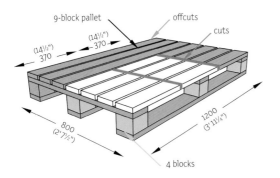

9-block pallet

offcuts

cuts

(14½")
370

(14½")
370

(14½")
370

800
(2'7½")

1200
(3'11¼")

4 blocks

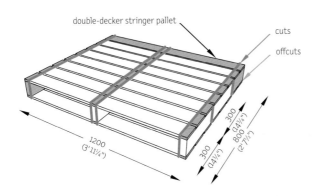

double-decker stringer pallet

cuts

offcuts

1200
(3'11¼")

300
(14¾")

300
(14¾")

800
(2'7½")

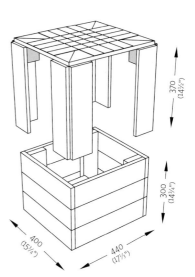

370
(14½")

300
(14¼")

400
(15¾")

440
(17⅓")

All measurements are given in millimetres and inches (to nearest fraction)

Method

1. THE CUBE: Taking the double-deck stringer pallet, saw the boards between the stringers in order to obtain 12 lengths of 400mm (15¾"). Remove the ends of the boards still attached to the stringers using a hacksaw, then saw the stringers into 4 lengths of 300mm (11¾").

2. Using ø3 (⅛") x 70mm (2¾") nails, nail the boards to the stringers, 3 boards to each side.

3. Take care with the positioning of the stringers when you fix the top boards. Two facing sides are attached to the width of the stringers, giving 2 sides of 400mm (15¾") and 2 of 440mm (17⅓") (see plan p.103, bottom right).

4. Use a sheet sander to sand each side, starting with 80-grit paper and finishing with 120, in order to obtain the smoothest possible surface.

5. <u>THE SEAT:</u> Taking the double-deck stringer pallet, saw 4 boards between the stringers to obtain 2 400mm (15¾") lengths and 2 440mm (17⅓") lengths. Using a mitre saw, make cuts at 45 degrees at both ends of each board.

6. Sand the 4 pieces with 80-grit sandpaper, then finish with 120-grit.

7. Using glue and ø2.2 (⁵⁄₆₄") x 40mm (1½") nails, fix the pieces to blocks salvaged from the block pallet. Take care to position the boards of equal length facing each other.

8. Prepare 2 x ø8mm (⁵⁄₁₆") dowel pins per block for the final assembly. Measure 20mm (¾") in from the sides of the block to mark the positions. With a ø9mm (²³⁄₆₄") wood bit, drill holes 2mm (¹⁄₁₆") deeper than the length of the dowel pins in order to leave room for the glue.

9. Paint the seat boards only. The poppy-red paint chosen here picks up the wine-coloured fillets on the jute webbing.

10. <u>WEAVING THE SEAT:</u> To determine the length of the webbing strips, measure the length of one of the boards, then add the width to allow for the webbing to wrap around the sides.

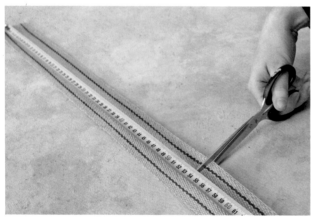

11. Cut several strips of webbing. Making sure they are evenly spaced throughout, check you have enough to cover before nailing them down.

12. Nail down the strips, in one direction first, using upholstery tacks. Tack the centre of the webbing first, then the edges, then fill in the rest.

13. Turn the seat over to weave the strips together, then tack the intersecting strips.

14. ASSEMBLING THE CUBE AND SEAT
Insert dowel pins in the blocks and cover them with chalk. Place the seat on the cube and press down in order to transfer the chalk marks. Drill. Check for fit, then squeeze glue into the holes to consolidate the structure.

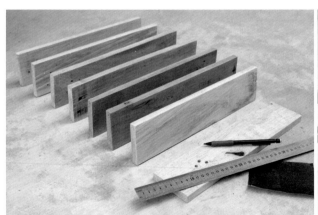

15. FINISHING THE POUFFE:
To finish the corners, salvage 4 740mm (2'5¼") lengths of board from the block pallet. Saw them in half to obtain 8 370mm (14½") lengths. Sand.

16. Using clamps, attach the finishing boards to the cube with glue and ø1.6 (¹⁄₁₆") x 30mm (1¼") round-head nails. Paint the corners to match the seat.

Le Fourbi Créatif de Macha
Marion Davaud, designer

Marion in 5 dates

1985: Born in Cholet, France.

2005: Gains diploma in interior design and window dressing from CEPRECO, Lille, France.

2008: Founds Le Fourbi Créatif de Macha.

2009: Testimonial from the Mission des Métiers d'Art/Pays-de-la-Loire.

2010: Undertakes eco-renovation project for her own house.

Marion Davaud is someone who works away quietly, discreetly salvaging, making, inventing. She has always created furniture from what lay to hand for her own living spaces. For Marion, recycling was not only a credo but also—in the beginning, for lack of means—a matter of necessity. 'Salvaging objects and furniture, converting and adapting them, I have become a true eco-designer over the years,' she explains. And so Le Fourbi Créatif de Macha was born.

How did you start designing furniture from wooden pallets?
In my daily work I am always using all sorts of salvaged materials, including wooden pallets. Pallets add value to a piece of furniture, the value of eco-design. They have the great advantage that you can use them to make bespoke, highly individual pieces.

What inspires your designs?
Furniture made from wooden pallets isn't just rough stuff that looks obviously salvaged. Using different forms and materials, you can create furniture and objects in a variety of styles. For the pouffe, adding another material was a natural step in order to make it more comfortable, hence the jute webbing. As for the bed head, I wanted to make a multi-purpose piece, one that was at once a bed head, bedside tables and lamps.

What are the pros and cons of working with pallets?
The pros are easy. Pallets are economical and easy to get hold of. And they offer so many creative possibilities. They can be used whole or taken apart and used for simple or complex constructions. And because they are cheap you have the leeway to make mistakes. For anyone wanting to try their hand at designing furniture or objects they make the ideal raw material.

What advice would you give to someone starting out as a designer of furniture and objects from pallets?
Don't look for perfection. Adapt your designs to suit the little faults in the pallets, which constitute their charm. And always remember to take into account how the wood may respond to changes of use and situation, depending on how well dried it is, how it has been assembled, the ambient temperature of a room, and the paint you use.

Le Fourbi Créatif de Macha

6, rue des Pêcheurs - 44140 Remouillé, France - Tel: +2 40 06 62 56
contact@lefourbicreatifdemacha.fr - www.lefourbicreatifdemacha.fr

Left: *Theatre* bed head (p. 58) ▪ Right: *Upholsterer's* pouffe (p. 100)

SUNDAY KITCHEN SHELVES

Utensils, spices and books all find their place on these practical and original kitchen shelves. Easy to make using any kind of wooden pallet, these sturdy little storage features would be equally at home in any other room in the house, from the bedroom to the living room.

The name carries with it nostalgic memories of childhood Sundays, and the delicious aromas of Sunday lunch ...

DESIGN INSPIRED BY:
ANA WHITE

MADE BY:
AURÉLIE DROUET

SUNDAY **KITCHEN SHELVES**

TOOLBOX

Tools

- Handsaw
- Hammer
- Clamps
- Sanding block and sandpaper
  (coarse and fine)
- Flat paintbrush

Materials

- 1 notched stringer pallet
  (here 1060 (3'5¾") x 1110mm (3'7¾"))
- Nails
- Black epoxy steel cup hooks
  (ø2.5 (³⁄₃₂") x 10mm (½"))
- Matt oil

Telling details: Useful extra storage space in the kitchen.
A shelving duo that would fit neatly in any room in the house.

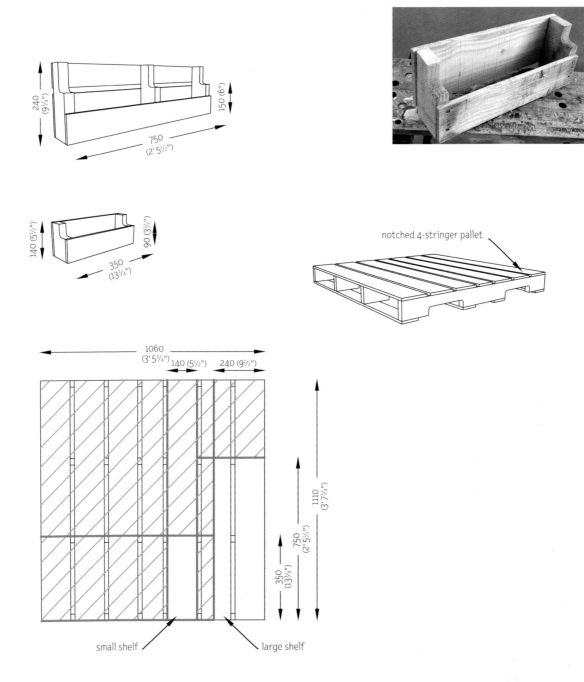

240 (9¾")

150 (6")

750 (2' 5½")

140 (5½")

90 (3½")

350 (13¾")

notched 4-stringer pallet

1060 (3' 5¾") 140 (5½") 240 (9½")

1110 (3' 7¾")

750 (2' 5½")

350 (13¾")

small shelf

large shelf

All measurements are given in millimetres and inches (to nearest fraction)

Method

1. To make two single shelves and one double shelf, saw the pallet up following the plan (previous page). You can adapt the number and size of the shelves according to your needs.

2. To make the shelf bottom, measure the openings of the cut sections.

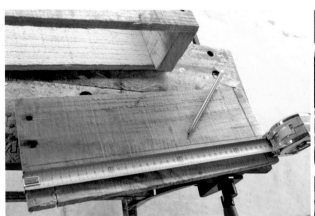

3. Transfer the measurements to an offcut from the pallet. Saw them with a handsaw to obtain a clean, accurate cut.

4. Clamp the two pieces together, then nail through the bottom into the thickness of the back board.

5. Turn the shelf over and nail through the front board into the thickness of the bottom.

6. Sand the shelf with coarse sandpaper to remove any roughness, then finish with fine paper to smooth the surface. A sanding block is useful for small areas and for slightly softening the corners.

7. Finish by applying a coat of oil with a flat paintbrush. Allow this to dry, then sand lightly with fine glass paper. Dust off, then apply a second coat. Leave to dry for at least 24 hours.

8. Cup hooks screwed to the bottom of the shelf will enable you to keep utensils to hand and free up drawer space.

PEACE AND LIGHT
WALL LIGHTS

Who would even think of salvaging a broken pallet? His keen interest
in the creative potential of scrap materials undimmed, with these
wall lights Philippe Daney demonstrates that the potential of the
human imagination is equally unlimited. One, two, three or more —
you can make as many as you like of these idiosyncratic lights,
arranging them vertically, horizontally or symmetrically. The
choice is yours.

There is an element of violence in these broken boards: imagine the
force needed to splinter and shatter them. Yet the glow shed by
the finished lights is a gentle one, like the sun breaking through
storm clouds — hence the name *Peace and Light*.

Philippe Daney's design uses LED lights, but small low-energy bulbs
would make a good alternative (see his *The Suitcase* floor lamp, p.143).

DESIGN:
PHILIPPE DANEY

PEACE AND LIGHT **WALL LIGHTS**

TOOLBOX
Tools

Tools

- Tools
- Handsaw
- Drill
- Sanding block + sandpaper (coarse and medium)
- Clamps
- Soldering iron + solder
- Slotted screwdriver
- Cable stripper

Materials

- 1 broken stringer pallet
- 3 square HB LED lamps + electric cable + 350mA LED power supply
- 6 small wood screws
- Screws and fixings to suit your walls

Telling details: Broken boards add an original touch.
Small low-energy bulbs can be used instead of LED lamps.

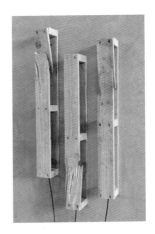

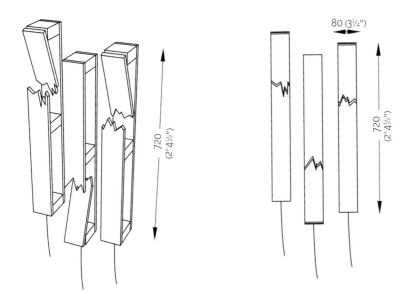

80 (3¼")

720
(2' 4½")

720
(2' 4½")

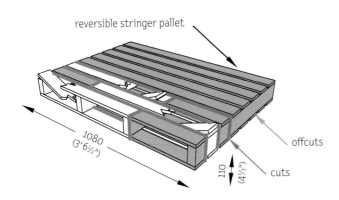

reversible stringer pallet

1080
(3'6½")

110
(4⅓")

offcuts

cuts

All measurements are given in millimetres and inches (to nearest fraction)

<u>Method</u>

1. Select the broken sections of the pallet and mark your cutting lines flush with the stringers. Saw.

2. Drill a hole in the back of each piece for fixing to the wall (the hole diameter will depend upon the wall fixings you are planning to use.)

3. Drill a hole for the electric cable in the middle of the section of stringer that forms the bottom of the light.

4. Drill through the central stringer where you want to position the LED lamp (this doesn't have to be centred). Sand the light with a sanding block, first with coarse sandpaper and then with medium to finish.

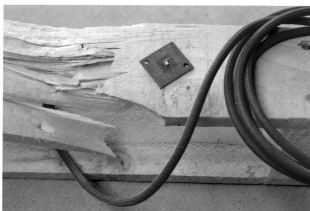

5. As the LED lamps are fixed to a wooden support they should not exceed 1W per lamp. Since the wattage is set by the power supply and number of lights, take care to choose the right one (here 350mA).

6. Strip the end of the cable and place the wires at the back of the LED. With a soldering iron, heat and apply the solder to the point of contact. Leave to cool for a few minutes before moving.

7. Thread the cable through the holes and screw the LED to the stringer. Connect up the wires with the power supply. **Safety warning:** *follow the instructions accompanying the LEDs*; if in doubt, consult a professional.

8. Hang the lights, using screws and fixings appropriate to the support.

Karl Zahn
Product designer

Karl Zahn in 5 dates

1981: Born in Burlington, Vermont, USA.

2003: Graduates from Rhode Island School of Design.

2005: First exhibition at the International Contemporary Furniture Fair, New York.

2009: Wins *Design Within Reach M+D+F* with his *Vladimir* mirror.

2009: Nominated for an FGI Rising Star award.

Karl Zahn is a freelance designer living and working in Brooklyn. After graduating from the Rhode Island School of Design, he moved to Copenhagen for several years to study Scandinavian design – the inspiration behind his creations, which are characterized by their careful balance between form and function. *Vladimir*, or the Pallet Mirror, is the fruit of his own personal research and experimentation.

Although in form the *Vladimir* mirror is reminiscent in some ways of nineteenth-century French mirrors, its origins are a world away from stucco and gold leaf. Conceived from two half-destroyed pallets, it expresses the infinite possibilities for re-use offered by this everyday packaging material.

Every pallet has its own story to tell, perhaps spanning thousands of kilometres from its place of origin to its destination. The 'scars' borne by each pallet bear witness to its own odyssey, branded into its fabric like the names and marks that identify it.

The name 'Dimare' that appears on the front of this mirror belongs to an Italian company specializing in tomato-based products. What's the connection with the mirror's name? Karl Zahn chose the name *Vladimir* as a reference to Bram Stoker's *Dracula*, inspired by Vlad Tepes, fifteenth-century ruler of Wallachia. The myth of the vampire, at once dead and 'undead', is here transposed to the life cycle of an inanimate object: useless and destined for destruction, the pallet has been endowed with second life. Tongue firmly in cheek, Karl Zahn relishes the analogy: the fixing marks on the surface of the wood 'are like the vampire's kiss', while the tomato sauce associated with the name Dimare reminds him (inevitably, perhaps) of 'human blood'.

Designpack Gallery

860 Manhattan Ave #4R - Brooklyn NY, 11222, USA - Tel: +1 415 202 3661
karl@oboiler.com - www.oboiler.com

1. *Vladimir* mirror (front view) ▪ 2. *Vladimir* mirror (detail) ▪ 3. *Vladimir* mirror (3/4 view) ▪ 4. *Vladimir* mirror (corner detail) ▪ 5. *Animal Box — Bull*: the *Animal Boxes* collection, lying somewhere between sculpture and totem, comprises six animals in all ▪ 6. Karl Zahn's Brooklyn workshop ▪ 7. Wood offcuts

CHARLOTTE
SHELF UNIT

Simple, practical and aesthetic: three words that sum up the *Charlotte* shelf unit. Adjustable and flexible, it appears here in its 'horizontal' format. Turn the modules through 45 degrees to create a vertical piece. Take it apart and put it together however you like, indeed – but do remember to keep it balanced.

With its play on modules, the *Charlotte* shelving unit pays modest tribute to the French architect and designer Charlotte Perriand, in whose work the idea of 'modularity' was a founding principle.

DESIGN:
M&M DESIGNERS

CHARLOTTE **SHELF UNIT**

TOOLBOX

Tools

- Drill (with ø9mm (²³⁄₆₄") wood bit)
- Handsaw
- Jigsaw
- Screw gun
- Orbital sander + sanding block + medium and fine sandpaper
- Clamps
- 1 long-reach paintbrush
- 1 round paintbrush
- 1 flat paintbrush

Materials

- 2 1060 (3'5¾") x 1060mm (3'5¾") double-wing stringer pallets
- 2 860 (2'9¾") x 1100mm (3'7⅓") reversible stringer pallets
- ø8mm (⁵⁄₁₆") dowel pins
- Wood glue
- 4 small double-threaded wood screws
- Coloured chalk
- Wood paint in the colour of your choice

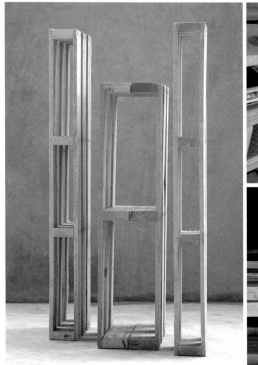

Telling details: A modular piece that can be customized to suit your needs.
Painting the internal surfaces adds depth to the ensemble.

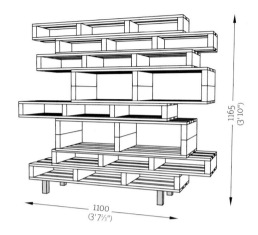

1165
(3'10")

1100
(3'7⅓")

2 double-wing
stringer pallets

cuts

offcuts

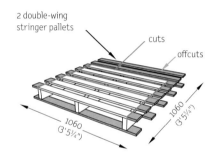

1060
(3'5¼")

1060
(3'5¼")

2 reversible
4-stringer pallets

cuts

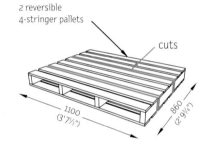

1100
(3'7⅓")

860
(2'9¾")

2 3-board modules

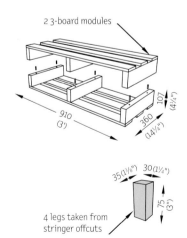

910
(3')

360
(14¼")

107
(4¼")

2 2-board modules

1100
(3'7⅓")

200
(8")

4 3-board modules

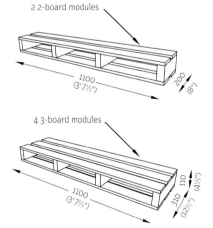

1100
(3'7⅓")

310
(12½")

110
(4⅓")

35(1⅜") 30(1¼")

75
(3")

4 legs taken from
stringer offcuts

All measurements are given in millimetres and inches (to nearest fraction)

Method

1. Following the plan, saw 3 modules (2 x 3 boards, 1 x 2 boards) from each of the 2 reversible stringer pallets. Use a jigsaw to cut the outer stringers.

2. Saw through the internal stringers with a handsaw.

3. Set aside 4 offcuts from the stringers (saw them between the boards) to make the legs.

4. Use the double-wing stringer pallets to make the taller modules. Remove the bottom deckboards.

5. Use pliers to remove any nails left in the stringers.

6. Saw off the wings of the top deck with the jigsaw.

7. Cut 2 3-board sections from each pallet, discarding the rest as offcuts.

8. Each tall module consists of 2 3-board sections placed on top of each other and fixed with dowel pins. Using a ø9mm (²³/₆₄") wood bit for ø8mm (⁵/₁₆") dowel pins, drill 2 holes in each stringer of one section, then insert the dowel pins.

9. Cover the dowel pins with chalk, place the second section carefully in position, then press down to mark the positions of the dowel pins.

10. Drill the holes in the second section, then check for fit. Squeeze some wood glue into the bottom of each hole to fix the structure.

11. Sand all the modules, ideally with a power sander.

12. On one of the shallow, 3-board modules, mark the position of one of the stringer offcut legs.

13. Fix the leg to the module with strong wood glue.

14. Clamp in position and leave to dry, then, for added strength, screw into the foot from the inner face of the module. Repeat with the other 3 legs.

15. Stack the 6 modules to form your shelf unit, alternating the shallow and deep modules, and taking care to keep the whole balanced.

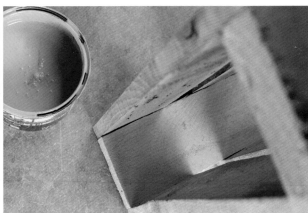

16. Paint the inner faces of the deep modules using a flat paintbrush and finishing with a round paintbrush. For the shallow, 3-board modules, where the inner faces are more awkward to reach, use a long-reach brush.

PETULA
PICNIC TRAY

With its tailored compartments, *Petula* recalls the coloured plastic meal trays of the 1970s — a classic revisited by Mr&Mlle™, who propose a playful variant in which it is up to you to create a jigsaw puzzle of offcuts. The shapes of the compartments? The arrangement of them? The base colour? All up to you, depending on your whim. In the living room or the garden, in front of the TV or al fresco, *Petula* makes impromptu meals a piece of cake.

Petula, its French designers remind us, is an anagram of plateau, which means not only 'tray' in French but also 'pallet deck' — a play on words that invites us to enjoy a fun and fuss-free *déjeuner sur l'herbe*.

DESIGN:
MR&MLLE™

PETULA PICNIC TABLE

TOOLBOX

Tools	Materials
■ Jigsaw	■ Pallet board offcuts
■ Holesaw	■ 2 sheets plywood, 350 (13¾") x 500 (19¾") x
■ Screw gun	5mm (¼") approx.
■ Nail and staple gun	■ Wood glue
■ Carpenter's pencil	■ Wood paint in the colour of your choice
■ 1 small round paintbrush	■ Colourless water-based kitchen varnish
■ 1 flat paintbrush	■ Plate, beaker, cutlery

Telling details: Practical compartments to hold cutlery, plate and beaker.
A playful picnic tray made from a mosaic of offcuts.

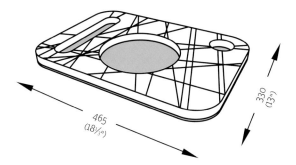

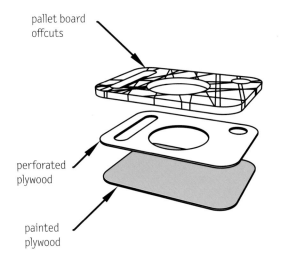

465
(18⅓")

330
(13")

pallet board
offcuts

perforated
plywood

painted
plywood

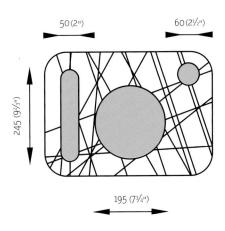

50 (2")   60 (2½")

245 (9⅔")

195 (7¾")

All measurements are given in millimetres and inches (to nearest fraction)

Method

1. Saw one of the plywood sheets to the dimensions of the tray: 330 (13") x 470mm (18½").

2. Using a plate, or lid, of the diameter and shape you require, draw in the position of the plate compartment as a guide for placing the offcuts.

3. Cut your board offcuts into small pieces. A variety of sizes, shapes and textures will add interest.

4. Compose your jigsaw puzzle on the plywood sheet, placing the offcuts side by side. Be creative with the positioning.

5. If necessary, trim them down with a jigsaw, or sander, to get a neat fit. Don't worry if the offcuts protrude over the edge: you will saw them off later.

6. Stick the offcuts to the plywood with wood glue. Leave to dry.

7. Turn the tray over to draw in the compartments for plate, beaker or glass and cutlery, as well as rounded corners.

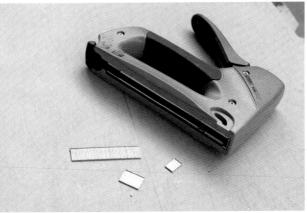

8. For a discreet finish, use a nail and staple gun and round-head nails.

9. Use the nail and staple gun to nail down all the edges of both the tray and the compartments, so making the tray more solid.

10. Cut around the sides of the tray with the jigsaw.

11. To saw the holes for the plate and cutlery compartments, drill a hole inside and against the line, with a wood bit diameter slightly bigger than that of your jigsaw blade.

12. Insert your jigsaw blade into this hole and carefully cut out your marked shape.

13. Use a holesaw to cut out the beaker or glass compartment.

14. Screw the second sheet of plywood, painted in advance, to the bottom.

15. Turn the tray over and saw off the surplus plywood sheet.

16. Seal the whole tray with colourless water-based kitchen varnish.

Mr&Mlle™
Bénédicte Lagrange and Jean-Marie Reymond

**Bénédicte
and Jean-Marie
in 6 dates**

1981: Birth of Jean-Marie
in Saint-Nazaire, France.

1982: Birth of Bénédicte
in Wissembourg, France.

2002: Jean-Marie and
Bénédicte meet as
students at the Ecole
des Arts Appliqués.

2006: Graduate in
interior architecture and
design from the Ecole
Pivaut, Nantes.

2007: Set up Mr&Mlle™.

2009: Spend six months
travelling in India and
Nepal.

Trained as industrial designers, Bénédicte Lagrange and Jean-Marie Reymond are now interior designers who have become increasingly interested in working with salvaged materials. Driven by concerns around the excesses of consumerism and of our production of household waste, they ask, 'Are we not in danger of losing our traditional attachment to objects?' Recycling, adapting and combining have become the hallmarks of their work. Adopting an ethical and pragmatic approach, they aim to 're-create the link between people and objects'—a link that is all the more powerful when people design their own everyday objects.

How did you start designing furniture from wooden pallets?
It was simple and complex at the same time. Simple, because pallets are made primarily from familiar material, wood. Complex because we were wary of falling into the over-simplistic clichés associated with pallets. We wanted to offer people designs that were accessible, in other words easy to reproduce, but that were also aesthetic and functional while respecting accepted standards, for instance for the height of different pieces.

What inspires your designs?
Everyday life! Our furniture is designed in response to the needs of our daily routines. We enjoy designing pieces that are useful and practical, but that are also stamped with a note of originality. In combining several functions in a single piece, the bedside table-light is an 'intelligent' piece of furniture that makes life simpler. The picnic tray is playful and fun to make, like a jigsaw puzzle. The desk project was different to work on, as it was the pallet that dictated the form. We wanted the pallet to be recognizable. First we designed the desk top, then we worked around it, trying to keep the lines as light as possible.

What advice would you give to someone starting out as a designer of furniture and objects from pallets?
Take care to choose the right type of pallet for each design. A desk needs a stronger base than a lamp, for example. And choose the right sections of wood to create the best effect. Watch out for knots and damaged areas that in the medium term could compromise the quality of your design.

Mr&Mlle™

6 bis, rue Noire - 44000 Nantes, France - Tel: +2 40 48 54 96
contact@mretmlle.com - www.mretmlle.com

Left to right: Where is Brian? coat stand (p.66) ▪ *Michel* desk (p.86)
Petula picnic tray (p.132) ▪ *Lisette* bedside table-light (p.156)

THE SUITCASE
FLOOR LAMP

Many people quail at the thought of making a lamp, largely because of the electrical side. Let us set your mind at rest, however: this design – requiring only the absolute minimum of materials, basic tools, assembly instructions that a child could follow and an easy electrical installation – is as simple as it is surprising. As well as bathing the room in a soft and welcoming light, *The Suitcase* floor lamp is also light and practical, and easy to move wherever you want it.

The name was inspired by both the shape of the lamp and the way it is used: a floor lamp the shape and size of a suitcase, designed to travel from room to room.

DESIGN:
PHILIPPE DANEY

THE SUITCASE **FLOOR LAMP**

TOOLBOX

Tools

- Handsaw
- Drill
- Orbital sander + sanding block
- Long-reach flat paintbrush
- Electrical screwdriver
- Cable stripper

Materials

- 1 520 (20") x 530mm (21") offcut from a double-wing stringer pallet (here taken from the *Cinchas* sun lounger)
- 1 pallet board offcut
- Socket
- Red electrical flex with switch and plug
- E27 LED light bulb (11W)
- Ø10mm ($^{25}/_{64}$") threaded pipe (20mm ($^3/_4$") long)
- Double-threaded wood screws
- Wood paint in the colour of your choice

Telling details: A light and versatile floor lamp, easy to move from room to room.
It needs few materials and is simplicity itself to make.

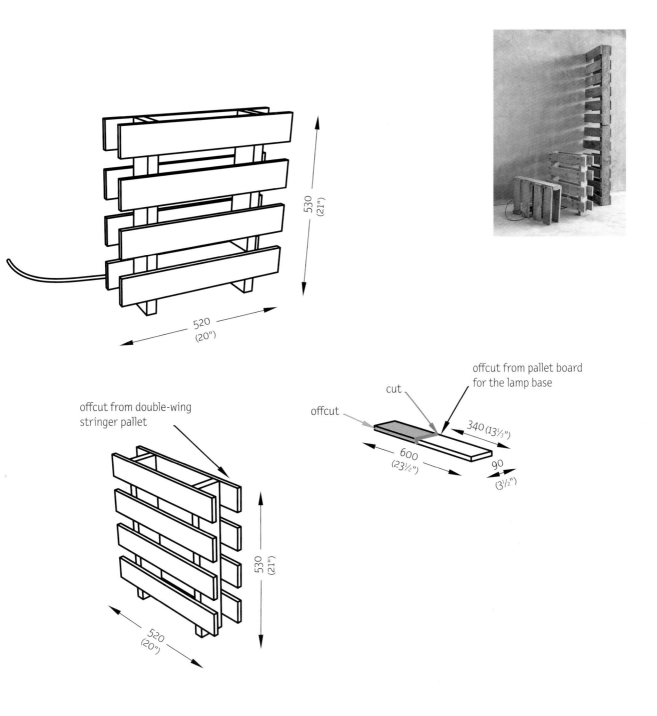

530
(21")

520
(20")

offcut from double-wing
stringer pallet

530
(21")

520
(20")

offcut from pallet board
for the lamp base

cut

offcut

340 (13⅓")

600
(23½")

90
(3½")

All measurements are given in millimetres and inches (to nearest fraction)

Method

1. Sand the outside of the offcut with the orbital sander and the inside with the sanding block.

2. To make the lamp base, measure the opening and mark the dimensions on your board offcut. Once cut, it should slot neatly into the space and hold the base rigid. Rule diagonals to mark the centre of the board.

3. Drill the board in the centre with a Ø10mm (²⁵/₆₄") wood bit.

4. Paint the lamp before going on to the electrical installation. Only the inner face is painted. Use a long-reach paintbrush for areas that are hard to reach.

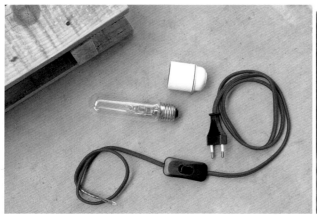

5. To make installation as easy as possible, manufacturers now sell flexes complete with switch and plug, sometimes even with the wires stripped. Tested for safety, they are very simple to use.

6. Thread the flex through the hole in the board, through the threaded pipe and then screw the threaded pipe into the base of the lamp socket.
Safety warning: *check against the instructions accompanying your appliance*; if in doubt, consult a professional.

7. If the wires have not been stripped, strip them back about 5mm (¼"). Insert them into the loosened terminals of the lamp core. Screw tightly with a flat screwdriver. Insert the lamp core in the base, then replace the body of the lamp socket.

8. Push, or screw, gently but firmly, the threaded rod of the lamp into the hole in the board to wedge it in place. Screw in the bulb and plug the lamp in.

LIZARD
GARDEN SEAT

A place for chatting or gossiping, flirting or thinking, musing or daydreaming, an inviting seat is an essential in every garden, public or private. Set in the shade of a tree, the *Lizard* seat offers the perfect spot for a quiet moment, alone or with friends.

Or choose a sunny spot, and bask in the sun like a lizard ...

DESIGN:
MARIE-NOËLLE SALAÜN
& AURÉLIE DROUET

LIZARD **GARDEN SEAT**

TOOLBOX

Tools

- Handsaw
- Hacksaw
- Cordless screwdriver
- Hammer
- Orbital sander + sanding block
- Clamps
- Flat paintbrush
- Soft cloth

Materials

- 3 800 (2'7½") x 1200mm (3'11¼") double-wing stringer pallets
- Stainless steel double-threaded wood screws
- Stainless steel nails
- Linseed oil
- Turpentine

Telling details: Cross-struts ensure solidity.
The seat can equally well be placed indoors or out.

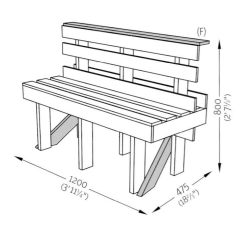

(F)

800
(2'7½")

1200
(3'11¼")

475
(18⅔")

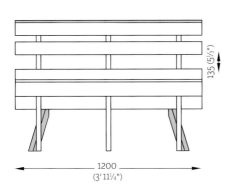

135 (5⅓")

1200
(3'11¼")

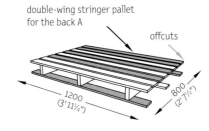

double-wing stringer pallet
for the back A

offcuts

1200
(3'11¼")

800
(2'7½")

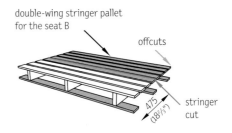

double-wing stringer pallet
for the seat B

offcuts

475
(18⅔")

stringer
cut

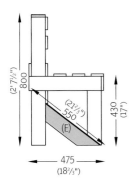

(2'7½")
800

(21⅔")
550

(E)

430
(17")

475
(18⅔")

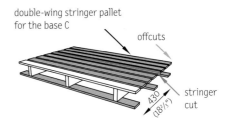

double-wing stringer pallet
for the base C

offcuts

430
(18⅔")

stringer
cut

All measurements are given in millimetres and inches (to nearest fraction)

Method

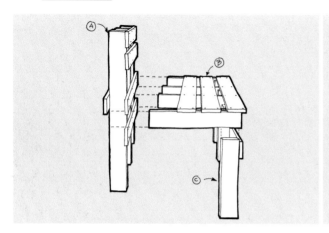

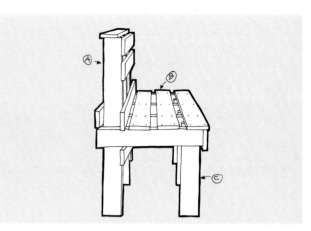

1. On pallet B, measure the desired depth, then remove the remainder of the boards to free up the stringers, following method 3, p.16. Remove all the boards of the bottom deck. On pallets A and C, remove surplus boards according to the appearance you want to achieve.

2. Flank the stringers of the seat (B) with two boards of the back (A) to a height of around 430mm (3"). Saw off the excess of the stringers. Measure out the height of the leg on pallet A and transfer it on to pallet C, then saw flush with a board to position the base (C) under the seat, flush with the boards.

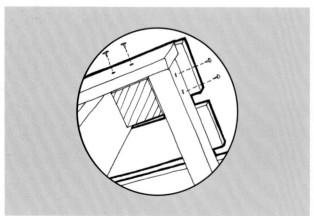

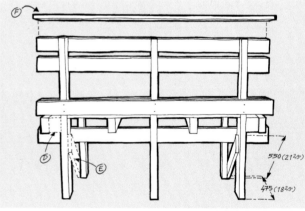

3. Fix the base to the seat by nailing offcuts from the stringers between the stringers at the far ends of the boards.

4. Fix the seat to the back by nailing the blocks to the stringers of both pallets (D).

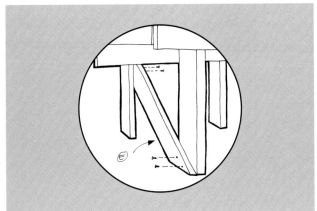

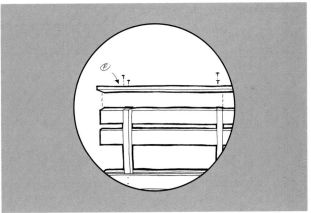

5. Make the cross-struts (E) from the boards removed earlier. Turn the bench over and position each strut against the outer face of the front leg and the inner face of the back leg. Attach the cross-struts to the stringers using stainless steel double-threaded wood screws.

6. Nail a board (F) along the top of the back to finish off. Sand the bench roughly to remove any splinters.

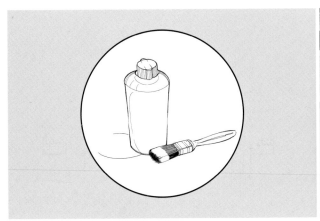

7. Linseed oil mixed with turpentine in equal parts is the traditional (and cheap) way of protecting wood while keeping a natural look. Apply with a brush, then rub off the excess with a soft cloth. Leave for 24 hours, then apply a second coat.

8. For a built-in herb garden, nail boards to the interior of the seat back and fill them with pots.

MODULOPAL™

Perched high above the rocky Atlantic shore, this cabin on stilts is a dream playhouse for children of all ages. Designed and built in 2008 by Philippe Besnard, this 8m² (86ft²) cube is built entirely of Euro pallets. Dubbed the Modulopal™, the cube has an interior measurement of 226cm (7'5") , in accordance with the anthropometric 'harmonious scale' of Le Corbusier's Modulor.*

In 2011, the cabin moved to Pornic, on the Breton coastline, where its owner, M. Hervouët, added salvaged materials to turn it into a fishing cabin. This unique construction has the advantages of being 'much lighter inside than traditional fishing cabins' and costing 'ten times less than a classic construction'.

Treated with borax before assembly, Euro pallets offer a solidity and mechanical strength that are robust enough to resist even the buffeting of Atlantic storms.

*Le Corbusier defined the Modulor, which he invented in 1943 as a means of reconciling imperial and metric measurements, as a 'range of harmonious measurements to suit the human scale, universally applicable to architecture and to mechanical things.'
Le Modulor, Editions de l'Architecture d'Aujourd'hui, translated into English as *The Modulor*, 1954.

1. Fishing hut at Pornic ▪ 2. Building the deck ▪ 3. Building the roof
4. The Modulopal™ logo ▪ 5. Design for an emergency shelter ▪ 6. Building the walls

LISETTE
BEDSIDE TABLE-LIGHT

Is this bedside light a lamp or a piece of furniture? *Lisette* has the design and function of a lamp, certainly, but it also works as a bedside table, as you can pile books inside it or perch your alarm clock on top of it. A multifunctional design that avoids the pitfalls of the bedside light that topples over every time you sleepily push your book on to the bedside table.

Taking their inspiration from the French word for a reading light, *la liseuse*, Mr&Mlle picked the name *Lisette* for this helpful beside table-light.

DESIGN:
MR&MLLE™

LISETTE BEDSIDE TABLE-LIGHT

TOOLBOX

Tools

- Hacksaw
- Jigsaw
- Holesaw
- Drill
- Detail sander
- Clamps
- Hammer
- Nail and staple gun
- 1 flat paintbrush
- 1 small round paintbrush

Materials

- 6 boards salvaged from 1 stringer pallet (here 1150 (3'9¼") x 1150mm (3'9¼"))
- Double-threaded wood screws
- Electrical flex, socket, switch and plug (often available as complete kits)
- Low-energy 40W light bulb
- Priplak™ opaque plastic, 185 (7¼") x 230mm (9¹⁄₁₆")
- Wood paint in the colour of your choice

Telling details: An integral space for books and an alarm clock.
A light bulb installed behind the opaque plastic lends this clever piece its dual function.

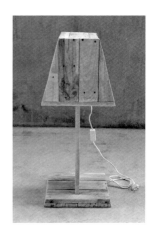

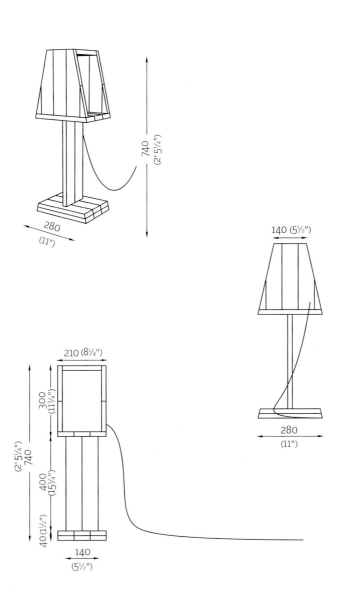

280
(11")

740
(2' 5¼")

140 (5½")

280
(11")

210 (8¼")

300
(11¾")

740
(2' 5¼")

400
(15¾")

40 (1½")

140
(5½")

All measurements are given in millimetres and inches (to nearest fraction)

Method

1. Dismantle the pallet according to method 3, p.16 and salvage 6 boards (1150 (3'9¼") x 75 (3") x 18mm (¾")). To make the base, cut 3 300mm (11¾") lengths from the first board and 4 225mm (8¾") lengths from the second board.

2. Clamp the 3 300mm (11¾") lengths together in order to mark out the notches for the light shaft.

3. Mark the positions of the notches by drawing a line lengthways down the centre of each of the outer boards, then another perpendicular to this extending to the inner edge. Use the depth of the boards (here 18mm (¾")) to measure the size of the notches, then cut them out with a jigsaw.

4. Cut 2 410mm (16¼") lengths to make the light shaft. Position them carefully over the base and transfer the measurements of the notches. Saw.

5. Slot the boards together using a hammer and tapping block.

6. Screw the base to the shaft, then strengthen it by screwing the 4 225mm (8¾") lengths (see step 2) to the bottom.

7. Use the jigsaw to cut the base at a 30-degree chamfer.

8. Screw the 3 300mm (11¾") boards to the top of the light shaft, then cut them at a 30-degree chamfer.

9. To make the sides of the light diffuser, cut 6 230mm (9¹⁄₁₆") lengths. Saw 2 of these lengths on the diagonal.

10. Screw the parts making up the diffuser to the light shaft, then nail the tops of the chamfered boards using a nail gun.

11. To close in the top of the diffuser, cut 2 185mm (7¼") lengths. Saw one of these in half lengthways, then cut the two visible edges at a 30-degree chamfer. Screw the first board centrally between the two uprights, then screw the half boards to each side. Sand.

12. Position a board inside the diffuser to separate the bookshelf from the light. Place it behind the light shaft, so that you can screw it in place from underneath. Prop a second board in position perpendicular to the first one and mark the cutting lines. Cut at a chamfer of 30 degrees. The light socket will be set into this piece.

13. Measure and mark out the position of the light socket, then drill the hole with a holesaw. Insert the light socket in the board, then screw the board to the inside of the diffuser.

14. Drill a hole in the side of the diffuser for the flex. Complete the electrical installation.
Safety warning: *check the colours of the wires against the instructions accompanying your appliance; if in doubt, consult a professional.*

15. Cut out the Priplak™ sheet and fix it to the board inside the diffuser using the staple gun. Priplak™ is tear-proof, tough and easy to use, but it should not touch the light bulb.

16. Paint the sides of the finished piece to emphasize its lamp-like appearance when viewed from the side. Sand lightly with fine sand paper, then apply a second coat.

BIBLIO'PAL
BOOKCASE

A bookcase is unlike any other piece of furniture. Casting off the serried ranks of dusty tomes that used to be its hallmark, it has evolved to become a showcase for much more than just books. With its array of interesting objects rubbing shoulders with books and storage boxes, CDs and magazines, this bookcase is a very personal reflection of the character of its owners. The principles on which it is assembled can easily be adapted to make your own unique bespoke bookcase.

The name *Biblio'Pal* is a fusion of *bibliothèque* ('bookcase' in French) and 'Modulopal', containing references to 'modules' and 'pallets'.

DESIGN:
MODULOPAL

BIBLIO'PAL BOOKCASE

TOOLBOX

Tools

- Handsaw
- Screw gun
- Pillar drill
- Ø14 ($^{35}/_{64}$") x 300mm (12") wood drill bit
- Angle-grinder
- Hammer
- Mallet
- Sledgehammer
- Orbital sander
- Clamps

Materials

- 8 800 (2'7½") x 1200mm (3'11¼") block Euro pallets
- 32 blocks
- Double-threaded wood screws
- 4 black plastic screw-in feet, 60 (2½") x 25mm (1")
- 2 6m (20') lengths of Ø10mm ($^{25}/_{64}$") rebar (to cut into 4 2m (6'6") lengths on purchase)

Telling details: Rebars give good stability.
The height of the shelves can be varied to accommodate different objects.

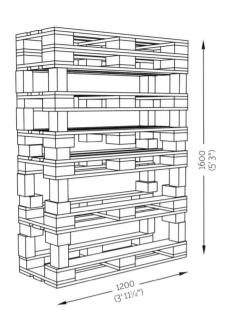

1600
(5' 3")

1200
(3' 11¼")

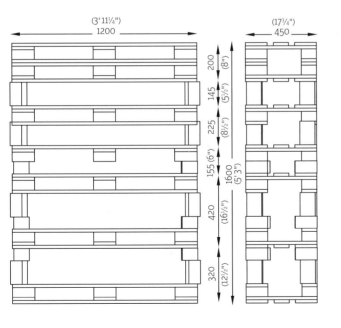

(3' 11¼")
1200

(17¾")
450

200
(8")

145
(5½")

225
(8½")

155 (6")

1600
(5' 3")

420
(16½")

320
(12½")

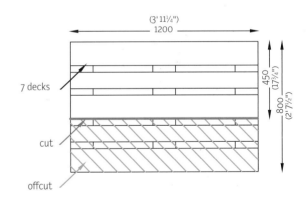

(3' 11¼")
1200

450
(17¾")

800
(2' 7½")

7 decks

cut

offcut

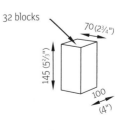

32 blocks

70 (2¾")

145 (5⅔")

100
(4")

All measurements are given in millimetres and inches (to nearest fraction)

Method

1. Saw the 7 pallets according to the plan, cutting alongside the central blocks to obtain pallets with 3 boards.

2. On 5 of the pallets, saw one of the bottom boards between the blocks.

3. On the remaining 2 pallets, remove the bottom boards and blocks according to method 2, p.16. Use an angle-grinder to cut off any remaining nails.

4. Salvage 23 blocks from the block pallets and offcuts, taking care to ensure they are uniform (a lengthy and painstaking job). Alternatively, see if you can find a friendly reconditioning firm to sell you a few blocks for a reasonable price.

5. Sand the pallets and blocks, using an orbital sander and coarse sandpaper.

6. To work out regular positions for the holes in the 7 pallets, make a drilling template. Saw up the 8th pallet as in step 3 (removing the bottom deck and blocks) and use the offcuts to make a framework for each corner.

7. Measure in 50mm (2") from the outer edges of the block to mark the position of the hole. Repeat for the other 3 corners, and transfer your measurements to the template.

8. Using a ø14mm (35/64") wood bit, drill through the template and the pallet. Repeat with the 6 other pallets, positioning the template with care to take into account the fact that every pallet is different, and the hole may become misaligned by a few millimetres.

9. Insert the 4 2m (6'6") rebars in the first section, a pallet turned upside down. Ask your supplier to cut the rebars for when you purchase them (it should be a free service.)

10. Mark the position of the hole, for drilling the blocks, by placing each block on top of the last as you work up the rebar. In this way you can work out the spacing for each one.

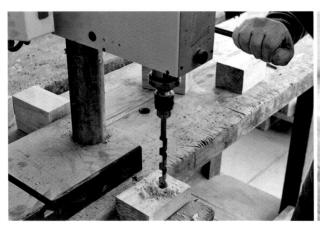

11. As drilling the blocks is a long job, a specialist pillar drill is recommended to ensure the drilling is kept straight. You can also use a drill fixed to a vertical support or with a drill guide attachment.

12. Following the indications on the plan and with a second person to help, stack the blocks and pallets on the rebars, adapting the height of the shelves by adding or removing blocks.

13. When you have stacked all the elements, lay the bookcase on the floor.

14. Use a sledgehammer to bend in the rebars at the bottom.

15. Attach the four black plastic feet.

16. Put the bookcase upright again, then use a clamp to fold down the rebars. One or two gentle taps with the sledgehammer may help.

Philippe Besnard
Furniture and cabin designer

Philippe in 6 dates

1955: Born in Tours, France.

1975: Graduates from the Ecole Supérieure des Beaux-Arts, Tours.

1986: Graduates from Promoca school of architecture, Nantes.

1990: First pallet project: an emergency shelter.

2007: Designs the Modulopal™ cube, using Euro pallets.

2009: Wins SEMA competition with the Modulopal Fauteuil Club [club armchair]™. Launches Modulopal Mobile Mobilier™.

From Monday to Friday, Philippe Besnard works full time for the Institut National de la Santé et de la Recherche Médicale (Inserm). The rest of the time he is a designer, working for over a decade exclusively with the standard Euro pallet, and creating everything from cabins to armchairs. His Modulopal™ venture started in 2007, when he built a cube: 'A cube is a volume of equal dimensions, repeated, which you can replicate as many times as you like.' It was a construction game that grew, with a variety of furniture designs under the trade name Modulopal™. 'Furniture falls into the category of needs that are more or less permanent and regular. It's a field in which wooden pallets can contribute responses that are individual and original, with an approach that can also be described as "built to last".'

How did you start designing furniture from wooden pallets?
When I began working with wooden pallets, I viewed them as modules, as part of a construction kit. After putting them together in plan mode, I wanted to relate them to the human body and to everyday or special uses. And so the day bed, armchair, banquette and other designs were born.

What have your inspirations been, from the beginning to the BiblioPal?
It's all a matter of stacking up decks and blocks in different conformations; of deliberately pushing the blocks out of true with each other in order to create the illusion of wonkiness in a piece that is in fact perfectly balanced. It asks the question: will the piece hold together, will it stand up? The answer is yes, but appearances may be otherwise.

What are the pros and cons of working with pallets?
Pallets are very 'democratic'. They're easy to find and they're affordable, or even free if they've been discarded. Any cons have to do with the roughness of their appearance, the awkwardness of their weight and the difficulty of taking them apart.

What advice would you give to someone starting out as a designer of furniture and objects from pallets?
Either someone needs the furniture, or the raw material prompts an idea. Either way, with the desire to do it, a few tools and a degree of space and time, it's fairly easy to get started. And you can always use the offcuts and rejects as firewood: nothing's lost, and the wood's come full circle!

Modulopal

Tel: +6 31 98 35 96 - modulopal@gmail.com
www.modulopal.com

Biblio'Pal bookcase (p. 164)

THE SHADOW'S SHARE Nº2
STANDARD LAMP

Standard lamp or wall light? Sitting both on the floor and against
the wall, this light fulfils a dual function. And it does so using offcuts,
so pushing the notion of salvage a stage further. Simple and
uncluttered in its design, when lit it creates a complex and intriguing
play of shadows, a subtly distorted shadowy doppelganger projected
on to the surface of the wall.

Hence the name ('Nº2' because this is the second Philippe Daney
lamp of this name).

DESIGN:
PHILIPPE DANEY

THE SHADOW'S SHARE N°2 STANDARD LAMP

TOOLBOX

Tools

- Handsaw
- Hammer
- Screw gun
- Orbital sander + sanding block
- Cloth

Materials

- 2 offcuts from 770 (2'6¼") x 370mm (14½") reversible stringer pallets (here from the *Charles-Edouard* armchair)
- 2 pallet boards
- Aluminum strip
- LED strip, connectors and transformer
- Methylated spirits
- Nails
- 12 small wood screws
- Angle bracket (length 20mm (¾"))

Telling details: A 100% recycled light made from pallet offcuts.
When fixed to the wall, the light creates intriguing plays of light and shade.

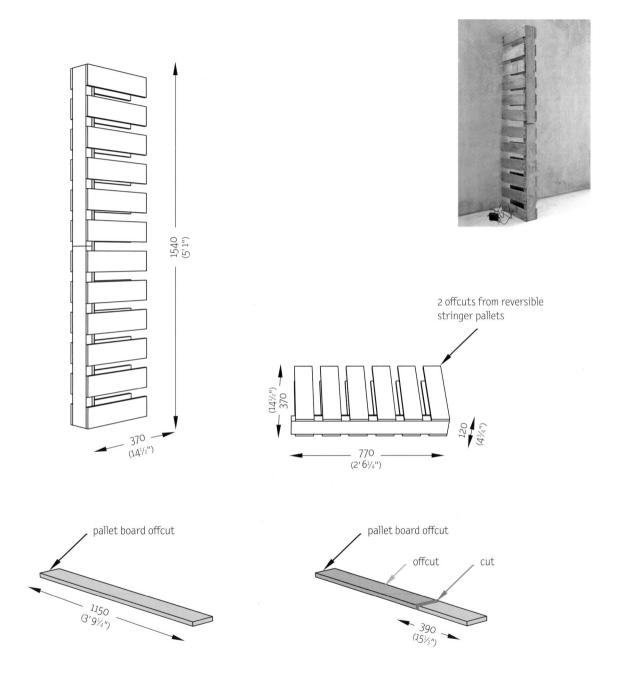

1540
(5'1")

370
(14½")

2 offcuts from reversible stringer pallets

(14½")
370

120
(4¾")

770
(2'6¼")

pallet board offcut

1150
(3'9¼")

pallet board offcut

offcut   cut

390
(15⅓")

All measurements are given in millimetres and inches (to nearest fraction)

Method

1. To assemble the structure of the lamp, position the 2 boards within the offcuts laid out on the ground. Mark off the excess board and saw.

2. Screw the boards to the stringers.

3. Strengthen any slightly 'rickety' boards by nailing them to the stringers. Sand the whole structure, using the sanding block for the interior and edges.

4. Cut a 1.4m (4'7¼") length of aluminium strip to serve as a support for the LED strip (which will not stick to wood), and also essential as heat insulation. Cut the LED strip to match, using the cutting guides on your product.

5. LED strip is self-adhesive and easy to install, requiring no soldering or electrical installation.

6. Wipe the aluminum strip with methylated spirits to ensure good adhesion, then carefully apply the LED strip. Connect the transformer. **Safety warning:** *follow the instructions with the LED strip; if in doubt, consult a professional.*

7. Screw the aluminium strip to the inner face of the lamp structure.

8. To ensure the stability of the lamp, attach it to the wall with an angle bracket.

LINE UP
DINING
TABLE

Extremely simple in construction, the
Line Up table can be made to any size.
Shown here in its extra large version, 2.4m
in length, it can easily be adapted to suit
your needs. The idea behind it was
to play with the shapes of the pallet to
create a wave of continuous lines,
from the feet to the top.

The name is taken from the lexicon
of surfing, in which 'Line Up' is used to
describe the area where the waves are
breaking – an evocative name to describe
the sleek lines that run the length of
this original table.

DESIGN:
M&M DESIGNERS

LINE UP DINING TABLE

TOOLBOX

Tools

- Handsaw
- Jigsaw
- Screw gun
- T-handle ratchet screwdriver
- Orbital sander + coarse and medium sandpaper
- Sanding block + 240-grit sandpaper
- Clamps
- Flat paintbrush (50mm (2")) for varnishing

Materials

- 4 identical 800 (2'7½") x 1200mm (3'11¼") heavy 9-block pallets
- 2 pallet boards (for the side-pieces)
- Double-threaded wood screws
- 11 60 (2½") x 160mm (6¼") perforated jointing plates
- 6 75 (3") x 100mm (4") x 60mm (2½") reinforced angle brackets
- Colourless water-based kitchen varnish

Telling details: The table's size can be adjusted to suit all needs.
Its sleek, uninterrupted lines run from the table top to the base.

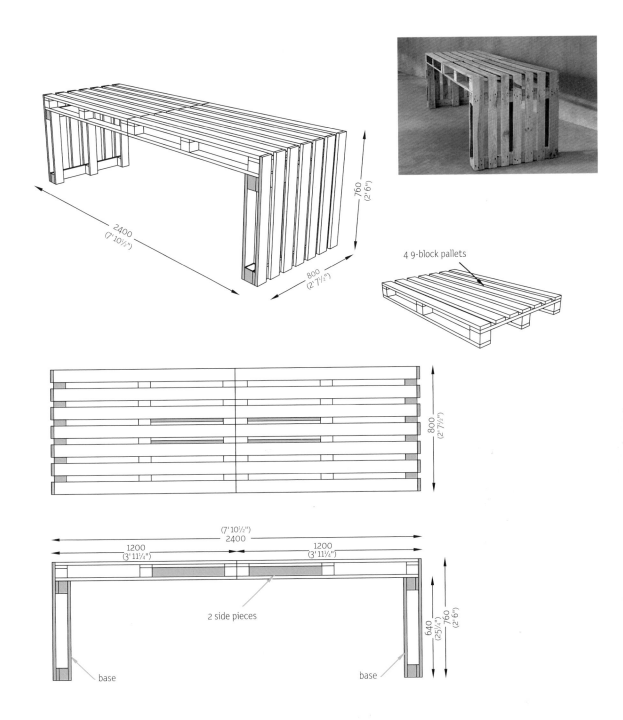

2400
(7' 10½")

760
(2' 6")

800
(2' 7½")

4 9-block pallets

800
(2' 7½")

(7' 10½")
2400

1200
(3' 11¼")

1200
(3' 11¼")

2 side pieces

640
(25¼")

760
(2' 6")

base

base

All measurements are given in millimetres and inches (to nearest fraction)

Method

1. Measure the height of the pallets (block plus boards) that will form the table top. Take care to measure both pallets.

2. Place the pallets that will form the 'legs' vertically, and transfer this measurement to the upper section of the boards, measuring from the central block.

3. Draw a line across the pallet to ensure a straight cut.

4. Using a jigsaw, saw along this line, slowly and steadily to achieve a perfectly straight cut. As this is not always easy with this tool, you may wish to use a rule or a straight board as a guide.

5. Turn the pallet over and mark the cutting line along the blocks of the lower section of boards.

6. Use the jigsaw to saw the boards flush with the central blocks.

7. Sand all the sections with an orbital sander, starting with coarse sandpaper and finishing with medium. As this is a piece of furniture for daily use, the sanding should be meticulous. Use a sanding block for edges and places that are hard to reach.

8. To assemble the table top, turn both pallets upside down and align them, clamping the blocks together.

9. Use 2 jointing plates to join the blocks on the table's outer edges.

10. If your screw gun will not fit in the space between the blocks, use a T-handle ratchet screwdriver. With its handy, ergonomically designed handle, this makes an ideal back-up tool for reaching awkward spots and for rapid screwing or unscrewing.

11. To ensure the top is completely rigid, use jointing plates to screw crosspieces to either side of the central blocks.

12. Position the legs on the upturned table top.

13. Clamp the legs in position, then attach them with 3 reinforced angle brackets at each end.

14. Apply a first coat of varnish to the outer surfaces of the table only (top and legs). Leave to dry, then sand lightly with 240-grit sandpaper. Dust off, then apply a second coat of varnish.

15. If the boards are too widely spaced, you can cover the top with glass or (a cheaper and more decorative solution) use mats to stop those teaspoons slipping through!

MOST Architecture
Paul Geurts and Saxon-Lear Duckworth

Paul and Saxon-Lear in 6 dates

1978: Paul Guerts born in Horst, Netherlands.

1980: Saxon-Lear Duckworth born in Harare, Zimbabwe.

2007: Graduation from Delft University of Technology.

2008: Meeting with Japanese architect Sou Fujimoto.

2009: MOST Architecture shortlisted for the Prix de Rome.

2010: First built commission.

When the Amsterdam advertising agency BrandBase commissioned them to design their offices in a typically long, narrow canal house, the Dutch architects Paul Geurts and Saxon-Lear Duckworth – who together form MOST Architecture – came up with a startling idea.

BrandBase wanted a temporary solution based on 'authentic and recyclable' materials. For the 245m² (2,637ft²) premises, MOST Architecture designed an interior made entirely from standard Euro pallets – 270 in all.

Tables, staircases, desks and platforms all evolved as the structure progressed, following the ways in which the pallets were placed and superimposed. The result was open offices in which each space has a separate function, whether meeting rooms, office spaces or reception area.

Guerts and Duckworth describe the space as 'an open and autonomous landscape made up of three layers'. The first layer is the existing space, painted white throughout in order to provide a uniform background to the pallets. The second consists of the pallets themselves, which define the internal spaces. And the third is formed by the decorative elements, with furniture, lights and stair rails all picked out in black.

Most Architecture - Paul Geurts & Saxon-Lear Duckworth

Westzeedijk 399 - 3024 EK Rotterdam, Netherlands - Tel: +31 6 45 15 26 88
info@mostarchitecture.com - www.mostarchitecture.com

1. Meeting room ▪ 2. Entrance hall ▪ 3. First-floor offices
4. Rest area ▪ 5. First-floor offices ▪ 6.Central staircase

CONTRIBUTORS' CONTACTS

- **Daney Factory/Philippe Daney**
13, rue de Bray - 35777 Cesson-Sévigné
Tel: +2 99 14 36 99
collectif@agence-daney.com/www.philippedaney.com

- **Edmond – Vintage furniture & objects** (chairs – photo p. 180)
Annabel Gueret
Loft des Mandarines - 37, quai de Versailles - 44000 Nantes
Tel: +6 07 04 98 25
annabel@edmond.tm.fr/www.edmond.tm.fr

- **Enzo Mari e Associati**
Piazzale Baracca 10-I-20123 Milan - Italy
Tel: +39 02 481 7315

- **Fabrice Peltier**
24, rue de Richelieu - 75001 Paris
Tel: +1 44 85 86 00/gallery@p-reference.fr
www.p-reference.fr/www.designpackgallery.fr/
www.allee-du-recyclage.fr

- **Karl Zahn**
860 Manhattan Ave #4R - Brooklyn NY, 11222 - USA
Tel: +1 415 202 3661
karl@oboiler.com/www.oboiler.com

- **Béa's blog**
bea4273@gmail.com
http://beatrice4273.canalblog.com

- **Le Fourbi Créatif de Macha/Marion Davaud**
6, rue des Pêcheurs - 44140 Remouillé
Tel: +2 40 06 62 56
contact@lefourbicreatifdemacha.fr/
www.lefourbicreatifdemacha.fr

- **Les P'tits Bobos – Children's furniture and decor**
(Wall mobile, cushions and quilt - photo p. 18)
Catherine Daunay
33, rue Léon-Jamin - 44000 Nantes
Tel: +2 40 48 05 40
contact@lesptitsbobos.fr/www.lesptitsbobos.fr

- **Les M&M Designers**
Martin Lévêque
44, rue Eeckelaers - 1210 Bruxelles - Belgique
kadiak29@hotmail.com
http://be.net/martinleveque

- **Mathieu Maingourd**
13, rue Barbe-Torte - 44200 Nantes
math_ology@hotmail.com
http://dopirate.free.fr

- **Modulopal/Philippe Besnard**
Tel: +6 31 98 35 96
modulopal@gmail.com/www.modulopal.com

- **Most Architecture**
Paul Geurts & Saxon-Lear Duckworth
Westzeedijk 399 - 3024 EK Rotterdam - Netherlands
Tel: +31 6 45 15 26 88
info@mostarchitecture.com/www.mostarchitecture.com

- **Mr&Mlle/Bénédicte Lagrange & Jean-Marie Reymond**
6 bis, rue Noire - 44000 Nantes
Tel: +2 40 48 54 96
contact@mretmlle.com/www.mretmlle.com

- **PGS – Palettes Gestion Services**
Centre Multi-Marchandises - BP 495 - 76807 Saint-Étienne-
du-Rouvray Cedex
Tel: +2 35 66 02 78
www.groupepgs.com

- **Studiomama/Nina Tolstrup**
21-23 Voss Street - E2 6JE London - UK
tolstrup@studiomama.com/www.studiomama.com

- **SYPAL - Syndicat de l'industrie et des services de la palette**
6, rue François Ier - 75008 Paris
Tel: +1 56 69 52 01
info@sypal.eu/www.sypal.eu

- **V33 – Paints**
Tel: +3 84 35 00 00
www.v33group.com

- **Photographer**
Jérôme Blin
Tel: +6 87 38 88 59
jerome.blin22@yahoo.fr/www.bellavieza.com

- **Styliste & Interior Deigner**
Marie-Noëlle Salaün
Tel: +6 80 78 74 40
salaun.m.n@gmail.com/www.marienoellesalaun.com